Written on the Wind
Collected Masonic Papers

by A.E. Waite

Foreword by Joseph Fort Newton
Edited by Michael R. Poll

A Cornerstone Book

Written on the Wind
Collected Masonic Papers
by A.E. Waite
Foreword by Joseph Fort Newton
Edited by Michael R. Poll

A Cornerstone Book
Published by Cornerstone Book Publishers
Copyright © 2023 by Cornerstone Book Publishers

All rights reserved under International and Pan-American Copyright Conventions. No part of this book may be reproduced in any manner without permission in writing from the copyright holder, except by a reviewer, who may quote brief passages in a review.

Cornerstone Book Publishers
Hot Springs Village, AR

First Cornerstone Edition - 2023

www.cornerstonepublishers.com

TABLE OF CONTENTS

Foreword v
Discourse on the Fellowcraft Degree 1
Some Deeper Aspects of Masonic Symbolism 7
Emblematic Freemasonry, Building
Guilds, and Hermetic Schools 29
The French Mystic and the Story
of Modern Martinism 46
Pillars of the Temple 93
London Morning Post's Attack on
Freemasonry 98
Universal Co-Freemasonry 114
The Life of the Mystic 121
The Word 129
The Templar Orders in Freemasonry 133
The Morality of the Lost Word 155

Foreword

Arthur Edward Waite - An Appreciation

ONE of the greatest masters of the field of esoteric lore and method of culture, by far the greatest now living, is Arthur Edward Waite, to whom it is an honor to pay tribute. In response to a number of requests, and as prelude to a lecture on the deeper aspects of Masonry, we offer a brief sketch of Brother Waite, with a statement of his conception of Masonry and its service to man in his quest of God. If these lines induce any of our readers to study his works, they will thank us for having put them in the way of so wise and skillful a guide, who is at once a poet and a mystic, the sum of whose insight, set forth on his latest page, is that:

> "All thoughts, all passions, all delights,
> whatever stirs this mortal frame,
> Are but the ministers of love,
> And feed his sacred flame."

By rare good fortune, as we think, our friend and teacher was born in America — in Brooklyn, New York — and on his father's side traces his descent back to the earliest settlers in Connecticut. His mother was English, belonging to the old family of Lovell. The family name, originally spelled "Wayte," was attached to the document authorizing the execution of Charles I, and it was probably the fact that the family found England a rather uncomfortable place in which to live after the Restoration that sent his ancestors across the sea. While the poet was still in his infancy his father died, and he was taken to England at the age of two. He has never returned to America —

a fact to be held against him, but for which we hope he will atone in a time not far away.

Educated privately, he began writing while still in his early teens, poetry being his first love. His first book, a volume of verse, was published in 1886. For ten years or more he pursued an active business life, as secretary and director of public companies, at the same time engaging in elaborate research in the fields of magic, occultism, and the esoteric side of religion and philosophy. How he found time to do both is not easy to know. He took the whole realm of mysticism for his province, for the study of which he was almost ideally fitted by temperament, training, and genius — and, we may add, by certain deep experiences in his own life, of which he rarely speaks, the glow of which one detects in all his work, and nowhere more vividly than in his latest book on "The Way of Divine Union." In later years, as the result of long study, he has come to deal only with higher mysticism, as totally separated from the magical, the psychical, and the occult.

Exploring a hidden world, he has brought to his task a religious nature, the accuracy and skill of a scholar, a sureness and delicacy of insight at once sympathetic and critical, the eye of a symbolist and the soul of a poet — qualities rarely found in union. Brother Waite does not write after our American fashion — "hot off the bat," as Casey put it — but in a leisurely manner, seeking not only to state the results of his research, but to convey somewhat of the atmosphere of the themes with which he deals. Prolific but seldom prolix, he writes with such lucidity as his subject admits of, albeit in a style often touched with strange lights and remote and haunting echoes. Much learning and many kinds of wisdom are in his pages; and if he is of those who turn down another street when wonders are wrought in the neighborhood, it is because, having found the inner truth, he does not ask for a sign.

Foreword

Always our brother writes with the conviction that all great subjects bring us back to the one subject that is alone great — the attainment of that Living Truth which is about us everywhere. He conceives of our human life as one eternal Quest of that Living Truth, taking many forms, yet ever at heart the same aspiration, to trace which he has made it his labor and reward.

Through all his pages he is following the tradition of this Quest, in its myriad aspects, finding in it the secret meaning of the life of man from his birth to his union — or reunion — with God who is his Goal. And the result is a series of volumes noble in form! united in aim, unique in wealth of revealing beauty, of exquisite insight, and of unequalled worth.

As far back as 1886, Brother Waite issued his study of the "Mysteries of Magic," a digest of the writings of Eliphas Levi, to whom Albert Pike was more indebted than he let us know. Then followed the "Real History of the Rosicrucians," which traces, as far as such a thing can be done, the thread of fact in that fascinating romance. Of the Quest in its distinctively Christian aspect, he has written in "The Hidden Church of the Holy Grail;" a work of rare beauty, of bewildering richness, its style partaking of the story told, and not at all after the fashion of these days. But the Graal Legend is only one aspect of the old-world sacred Quest of the truth most worth finding, uniting the symbols of chivalry with the forms of Christian faith.

Masonry is another aspect of that same age-long Quest; and just as Brother Pound has shown us the place of Masonry among the institutions of humanity, and its meaning as such, so Brother Waite shows us the place of Masonry in the mystical tradition and aspiration of mankind. No one may ever hope to write of "The Secret Tradition in Masonry" with more insight and charm, or a touch assured and revealing, than this gracious scholar to whom Masonry perpetuates the Instituted Mysteries of antiquity, with much else derived from innumerable storehouses of treasure. What then are the marks of this eternal Quest, whether its legend be woven about a Lost Word, a design left unfinished by a Master Builder, or, in its Christian form, about the Cup of Christ?

They are as follows: first, the sense of a great loss which has befallen humanity, making us a race of pilgrims ever in search of that which is lost; second, the intimation that what was lost still exists somewhere in time and the world, although deeply buried; third, the faith that it will ultimately be found and the vanished glory restored; fourth, the substitution of something temporary and less than the best, but never in a way to adjourn the quest; and fifth, the felt presence of that which is lost under veils and symbols close at hand. What though it takes many forms, it is always the same quest, and from this statement of it, surely, we ought to see that Masonry has a place in the greatest quest which man has pursued in the midst of time. Our Order is thus linked with the shining tradition of the race, having a place and a service in the culture of the life of the soul, leading men in the search for God, if happily they might feel after Him, and find Him, though He is not far from any one of us.

But this is a long and difficult quest, and we must walk carefully, lest we trip and fall into the pits that beset the path. Brother Waite warns us against the dark alleys that lead nowhere, and the false lights that lure us to ruin, and he protests against those who would open the Pandora's Box of the Occult on the altar of Masonry. After a long study of occultism, magic, omens, talismans, and the like, he has come to draw a sharp line between the occult and the mystical — and therein he is wise. From a recent interview with him in regard to these matters in an English paper, we may read:

> "There is nothing more completely set apart from mysticism than that set of interests and things called occultism. Occultism is concerned with the idea that there were a number of secret sciences handed down from the past, and which, roughly speaking, represented the steps toward the attainment of abnormal power by man, corresponding to the idea of Magic. Magic, of course, meant many things: it meant the power obtained by man as a result of dealing with spirits, raising the spirits of the dead, everything that we understand by the supposed efficacy of talismans, and all that is comprehended in the word Astrology. My interest in these things has been purely historical and critical.
>
> Occult and psychical research does help, of course, to show that the purely materialistic interpretation of things does not cover the whole field. It shows a residue of experience which points to the existent of powers beyond the norm of man, some of them maleficent, others innocent in themselves, of which the student may take account. Unfortunately, I have known too many who follow these things as the be-all and end-all of their interests. I know others also, and many, to whom the exaggerated pursuit has spelt not less than ruin. I mean, morally and spiritually. I know, for the rest, that they reach no real term; very soon they come up against a dead wall."

Here are grave and wise words, spoken out of full knowledge of history and fact, and he is wise who heeds them. It is no theological bias of any sort, but the profound fallacy of the occult, and its danger to the highest life and character, that has moved us more than once in these pages to utter a like warning to those who would turn aside from the historic highway of the soul to follow a will-of-the-wisp into the bog. If Masonry forsakes its Great Light to follow these wandering tapers, it too will fall into the ditch. But to listen to Brother Waite:

> "Symbolism is sacramental. To me all visible things are emblems. When you come to think of it, is it not true that all the workings of the human mind are in the form of symbols? These symbols are truly representative and not mere figments of the mind, and to get at the reality behind the symbol is the aim of the mystic. The theory of mysticism is that the voice of God is within, and that the soul has to enter into the realization that God is within. The question is whether that realization can be fully achieved in this life. All, or nearly all, the great mystics, held that they only approximated it. The absolute vision and union lie very far away — so the quest of the Lost Word goes on, ever on.
>
> Mysticism is not a way of escape, either from oneself or the world. It is by the realization of the indwelling of God in all around, and within, in things animate and inanimate, and most of all in the soul of man, that we attain to knowledge of God — in so far as we attain it in this life. Thus, it is not a path of escape from the world, as the old ascetics imagine, but by finding God in the world, the ideal in the real, one with the ideal within us, that we attain to union with God. We are sacraments to ourselves. A man building a house would perhaps be surprised if you told him that he is not merely building bricks and stones, but that he

is trying to bring into being something of the idealism in his own nature, but if he could be brought to understand that, would it not give a new glory to his work?"

Thus mysticism, as here presented, is practical common sense — bringing to the humblest task the highest truth to lighten and transfigure our labor. Time does not permit us to speak of the poetry of Brother Waite, though some think his best work has been done in that field. He himself thinks of his poetry as "light tongued rumors and hints alone of the songs I had hoped to sing." We must, however, mention his drama "The Morality of the Lost Word," which may be found in his poems, recently collected in two noble volumes, and we bespeak for it a long study. At another time we shall speak of the poetry of our friend to whom the world is ever an infinite parable, giving at present only the following lines as a hint of his poetic purpose and power:

"In the midst of a world full of omen and sign, impelled by the seeing gift. On auspice and portent reflecting, in part I conjecture their drift; I catch faint words of the language which the world speaks far and wide. And the soul withdrawn in the deeps of man from the birth of each man has cried. I know that a sense is beyond the sense of the manifest Voice and Word. That the tones in the chant which we strain to seize are the tones that are scarcely heard; While life pulsating with secret things has many too deep to speak, and that which evades, with a quailing heart, we feel is the sense we seek: scant were the skill to discern a few where the countless symbols crowd, to render the easiest reading, catch the cry that is trite and loud."

For the rest, we confess a great debt to our dear friend and Brother across the great waters, divided by distance but very near in thought and sympathy and regard; a man of pure and lofty spirit, tolerant of mind, noble of nature, in all ways a true Master Mason — and one who does not forget "that best portion of a good man's life, the little, nameless, unremembered acts of kindness and of love."

JOSEPH FORT NEWTON
The Builder Magazine
1916

Written on the Wind
Collected Masonic Papers

Discourse on the Fellowcraft Degree

BRETHREN of the Order, and those among you in particular who have been received recently among us, there is no period too early to conceive a just and commensurate notion of the great institution to which we belong, and in which we have been incorporated as a part of its living body. It is desirable, in the first place, that we should understand certain intimations which occur in the Grade of Neophyte and in that of Fellow Craft. They are open on their surface to misconstruction, and did we afterwards pursue our research into the history of Emblematic Freemasonry, it might even be thought that they were untrue unless we carried them further than is commonly done. Moreover, in the absence of such research, they might come to be regarded as so many figures of speech.

The Entered Apprentice is told at an early stage of his experience that the Order possesses great and inestimable privileges as well as those secrets and mysteries concerning which he is sworn to inviolable secrecy. You will observe that the privileges are enumerated separately from the secrets, though the latter stand also for privileges. Among these I will particularize the Signs and Words of the successive Degrees. The privileges imparted by these include the right of entrance to a Lodge, as a guest or subscribing member. They are the titles of our initiation and assuredly they are more than valuable after their own kind, but they do not respond in themselves to the very wide claim which I have mentioned. I conceive therefore that there are other privileges. These are not, however, to be identified with the things implied by the great principles of the Order, precious as are the latter to our hearts, and advantageous as it must ever be to dwell within a circle of fellowship which recognizes the principles of solidarity and will at need extend them in good will to us. They are not in the category of those things which we seek to reserve to worthy men alone. They are rather the marks, seals, and characters which it is our sacred duty to display and by which Masonry is known all over the world in its practice of beneficence, benevolence, and fraternity, by the love of moral truth and by the truth which abides in honor. I conclude, therefore, that the reference to inestimable privileges is itself in the nature of a mystery and covers things which do not exactly appear on the literal side of our rituals. This is the first point which I am now seeking to commemorate.

The second is concerned more especially with the obligation of the Neophyte Grade in which the Candidate is pledged to hele, conceal, and never reveal the secret art and hidden mysteries of Masonry. I believe that after a little reflection I shall carry with me the concurring voice of every Brother amongst us, if I say that this pledge, with the penalties attached thereto, must cover more than the simple signs, tokens, words and procedure which takes place in our Lodges, or too elaborate machinery may be thought to be put in motion than the-end appears to require. Hence again it seems certain that the reference to secret arts and hidden mysteries is itself in a mystery and covers things which do not precisely appear on the literal surface of our Rituals. This is the next point which I am seeking to commemorate here.

For the third, we must pass from the Grade of Initiate or Neophyte to that of Fellow Craft, in which there is a brief but singularly pregnant account of that which was attained by the Candidate when he was made an Entered Apprentice; and of that which he is expected to perform in his new capacity as a Craftsman. In the one it is pointed out that he has made himself acquainted with the principles of moral truth and virtue. Now, this is literally true, subject to a single reserve: as one newly admitted, he was not intended to be tried beyond his strength: the principles which he is said to have acquired were communicated to him without action on his own part, but he was left in the First Degree to reflect upon them. They are actually the root matter and sum total of moral truth and all-natural virtue. It is otherwise in the Degree of Fellow Craft. There it is assumed that the Masonic horizon has opened before and about him, and that he is prepared to enter an almost immeasurable region. He is accordingly advised that he is expected to make the liberal arts and sciences his future study, and that he is permitted to extend his research into the hidden mysteries of Nature and science. Once again, this is an intimation which covers much more than appears on the literal surface and is a mystery which is expressed shortly but not explained in our Rituals. Here is the third point which I am now seeking to commemorate.

Let us see if there is any direction in which we can turn for a little light on these problems, and as it so happens, we shall not have to go outside the Lodge itself.

On his first entrance into Freemasonry the newly received Brother will perceive that he has come into a world of emblems or symbolism, and that whatsoever takes place therein has a meaning behind it which is by no means indicated invariably on the surface. Sometimes, and indeed frequently, there is more than one inward meaning, depending on the point of view from which it is approached. The Lodge is an eloquent example of this truth. When the door opens for the Candidate, he enters an institution which has its branches spread over the four quarters of the globe. It may be a very small Lodge: it may be a Lodge of poor Brothers only: but whosoever is received therein is recognized through the Masonic world, in all countries and among all peoples. But there is more even than this: however humble in its appointments and proportions, that Lodge is a Microcosm, a symbol, a speaking likeness of universal Freemasonry. It represents also and contains the life of Masonry, and the Ceremony of his initiation integrates the new-made Brother in that peculiar quality of life which is the principle and essence of the Order. He becomes part of an organic whole. In the third place, the Lodge is held to represent the three dimensions of space—that is to say, the universe itself as a cosmos: in length from East to West, in breadth between North and South, in depth from the surface to the center, and even as high as the heavens.

It is therefore as if the Candidate on his initiation had been born anew into the universe, or that a door had opened to admit him into another cosmos. He comes with his eyes dim and with a restraint about him; he is kept for a considerable period in a state of darkness and bondage: ultimately, he is instructed, and that which he finds about him is truly the symbolic representation of a new world. For him at that moment all things seem to be renewed, and it is very soon after this strange and wonderful experience that he is given a key to the meaning. He is told that he is the cornerstone of a new foundation, from which he must build up himself after another and higher manner. In other words, he must remake his inward nature according to the perfection of the standard which is prescribed by Masonry. It is a moral standard in respect of his dealings with his brethren and with mankind at large. It is a spiritual standard in respect of his duty towards God, and through obedience thereto it is hoped, held, and known that he will ascend to the home of the spirit in the heavenly kingdom, by means of the ladder of Jacob, the successive rounds of which are called by many names, but chief among these are faith, hope and charity. It follows that he has a two-fold work to perform, but it is all in the training of himself. If he is successful, the result will be perfect in its parts and honorable to the builder. From this point of view, the just, perfect, and regular Lodge is also a symbol of the man in that state which he is called to attain.

Now, the word initiate, with which we are so familiar in Masonry, signifies a person who has made a new beginning, who has entered a path of experience heretofore untraveled. Its equivalent in other orders and fraternities is the word Neophyte. The Neophyte is also one who has made a new beginning and the term, which is Greek in its origin, signifies him who is reborn, a new plant, one who is remade. In the old, instituted mysteries, like those of Samothrace, of Egypt and of Eleusis, the Candidate was regenerated or reborn—he was otherwise transferred or grafted—at the beginning of his experience, and afterwards he passed through successive stages of a new life till he attained the culminating Grade. It was the same experiment as that of Craft Masonry, in which the Candidate—as an Entered Apprentice—lays the foundation stone of that new building which is himself, raises a super structure according to the law and order that Masonry has imposed upon him, continues the erection as a Craftsman, in which Degree the mysteries of Nature and science, recommended to his study, are mysteries of God and the estimation of His wonderful works till at last he puts on the capstone when the Lodge is open in the Sublime Grade of Master.

Our secret art is therefore an art of life, an art of perfection, an art of creation according to a prescribed standard recognized in Masonry: our hidden mysteries are those of our own relations to God, man, and the universe, that we may be enabled to fulfill by Masonry the higher law of our being. The inestimable privileges of Masonry include those of its symbolism, the study of which is for our instruction in this high mode of self-building. The arts and mysteries which we are pledged to conceal from the profane are also those of the peculiar law of life in Masonry by which these ends can be reached. Those who are outside the Lodge must come within it if they desire to share in that life. It is incommunicable beyond the mystic circle, for the simple reason that it is life itself and not one of its substitutes. While therefore we are properly pledged concerning it, there is something which we could not impart even if we tried. In some of the old mysteries, from which we are indirectly descended, initiation and its sequels meant real instruction in this subject, and several of our most suggestive intimations are reflections from that remote source.

And seeing that the Grade of Master Mason is not so much a reflection as the very root, essence and quintessence, of those mysteries, and may be shortly described as an experiment in the deep mystery by which the soul passes through mortal life towards that life in God which is the end of all the mysteries, it comes about in this manner, my Brethren, that we are incorporated with all the great orders and sodalities of the distant past and are therefore justified when we say that the meaning of our Masonic Badge is more ancient than the Golden Fleece and that our honorable institution — though under many transformations — has subsisted from time immemorial.

SOME DEEPER ASPECTS OF MASONIC SYMBOLISM

PART I

THE SUBJECT which I am about to approach is one having certain obvious difficulties because it is outside the usual horizon of Masonic literature, and requires, therefore, to be discussed with considerable care, as well as with reasonable prudence. Moreover, it is not easy to do full justice within the limits of a single lecture. I must ask my brethren to make allowance beforehand for the fact that I am speaking in good faith, and where the evidence for what I shall affirm does not appear in its fullness, and sometimes scarcely at all, they must believe that I can produce it at need, should the opportunity occur. As a matter of fact, some part of it has appeared in my published writings.

I will introduce the question in hand by a citation which is familiar to us all, as it so happens that it forms a good point of departure: — "But as we are not all operative Masons, but rather Free and Accepted or speculative, we apply these tools to our morals." With certain variations, these words occur in each of the Craft Degrees, and their analogies are to be found in a few subsidiary Degrees which may be said to arise out of the Craft — as, for example, the Honorable Degree of Mark Master Mason. That which is applied more specially to the working implements of Masonry belongs to our entire building symbolism, whether it is concerned with the erection by the Candidate in his own personality of an edifice or "superstructure perfect in its parts and honorable to the builder," or, in the Mark Degree, with a house not made with hands, eternal in the heavens, or again with Solomon's Temple spiritualized in the Legend of the Master Degree.

A System of Morality

It comes about in this manner that Masonry is described elsewhere as "a peculiar system of morality, veiled in allegory and illustrated by symbols." I want to tell you, among other things which call for consideration, something about the nature of the building, as this is presented to my mind, and about the way in which allegory, symbols and drama all hang together and make for one meaning. It is my design also to show that Craft Masonry — incorporates three less or more distinct elements which have been curiously inter-linked under the device of symbolic architecture. That inter-linking is to some extent artificial, and yet it arises logically, so far as the relation of ideas is concerned.

There is, firstly, the Candidate's own work, wherein he is taught how he should build himself. The method of instruction is practical within its own measures, but as it is so familiar and open, it is not, properly speaking, the subject-matter of a Secret Order. There is, secondly, a building myth, and the way it is put forward involves the Candidate taking part in a dramatic scene, wherein he represents the master-builder of Masonry. There is, thirdly, a Masonic quest, connected with the notion of a Secret Word communicated as an essential part of the Master's Degree in building. This is perhaps the most important and strangest of the three elements; but the quest after the Word is not finished in the Third Degree.

The First Degree

Let us look for a moment at the Degree of Entered Apprentice, and how things stand with the Candidate when he first comes within the precincts of the Lodge. He comes as one who is "worthy and well recommended," as if he contained within himself certain elements or materials which are adaptable to a specific purpose. He is described by his conductor as a person who is "properly prepared." The fitness implied by the recommendation has reference to something which is within him, but not of necessity obvious or visible on his surface personality. It is not that he is merely a deserving member of society at large. He is this, of course, by the fact that he is admitted; but he is very much more, because Masonry has an object in view respecting his personality — something that can be accomplished in him because of his fellowship in the Brotherhood, and by himself. As a matter of truth, it is by both. The "prepared" state is, however, only external, and all of us know of what it precisely consists.

Now the manner of his preparation for entrance to the Lodge typifies a state which is peculiar to his ward position as a person who has not been initiated. There are other particulars into which I need not enter, but it should be remarked that in respect of his preparation he learns only the meaning of the state of darkness, namely, that he has not yet received the light communicated in Masonry. The significance of those hindrances which place him at a disadvantage, impede his movements, and render him in fact helpless, is much deeper than this. They constitute together an image coming out from some old condition by being unclothed therefrom — partially at least — and thereafter of entering a condition that is new and different, in which different light is communicated, and another vesture is to be assumed, and, ultimately, another life entered.

The Meaning of Initiation

In the first Degree the Candidate's eyes are opened into the representation of a new world, for you must know, of course, that the Lodge itself is a symbol of the world, extending to the four corners, having the height heaven above and the great depth beneath. The Candidate may think naturally that light has been taken away from him for the purpose of his initiation, has been thereafter restored automatically, when he has gone through a part of the ceremony, and that hence he is only returned to his previous position. Not so. The light is restored to him in another place; he has put aside old things, has come into things that are new; and he will never pass out of the Lodge as quite the same man that he entered. There is a very true sense in which the particulars of his initiation are in analogy with the process of birth into the physical world. The imputed darkness of his previous existence, amidst the life of the uninitiated world, and the yoke which is placed about him is unquestionably in correspondence with the umbilical cord. You will remember the point at which he is released therefrom — in our English ritual, I mean. I do not wish to press this view, because it belongs of right, in the main, to another region of symbolism, and the procedure in the later Degrees confuses an issue which might be called clear otherwise in the Degree of Entered Apprentice. It is preferable to say that a new light — being that of Masonry — illuminates the world of the Lodge in the midst of which the Candidate is placed; he is penetrated by a fresh experience; and he sees things as they have never been presented to him before. When he retires subsequently for a period, this is like his restoration to light; in the literal sense he resumes that which he set aside, as he is restored to the old light; but in the symbolism it is another environment, a new body of motive, experience, and sphere of duty attached thereto. He assumes a new vocation in the world.

The question of certain things of a metallic kind, the absence of which plays an important part, is a little difficult from any point of view, though several explanations have been given. The better way toward their understanding is to put aside what is conventional and arbitrary — as, for example, the poverty of spirit and the denuded state of those who have not yet been enriched by the secret knowledge of the Royal and Holy Art. It goes deeper than this and represents the ordinary status of the world, when separated from any higher motive — the world-spirit, the extrinsic titles of recognition, the material standards. The Candidate is now to learn that there is another standard of values, and when he comes again into possession of the old tokens, he is to realize that their most important use is in the cause of others. You know under what striking circumstances this point is brought home to him.

Entered, Passed, Raised

The Candidate is, however, subjected to personal experience in each of the Craft Degrees, and it calls to be understood thus. In the Entered Apprentice Degree, it is because of a new life which he is to lead henceforth. In the Fellowcraft, it is as if the mind were to be renewed, for the prosecution of research into the hidden mysteries of nature, science, and art. But in the sublime Degree of Master Mason, it is in order that he may enter fully into the mystery of death and of that which follows thereafter, being the great mystery of the Raising. The three technical and official words corresponding to the successive experiences are Entered, Passed, and Raised, their Craft — equivalents being Apprentice, Craftsman and Master — or he who has undertaken to acquire the symbolical and spiritualized art of building the house of another life; he who has passed therein to a certain point of proficiency, and in fine, he who has attained the whole mystery. If I may use for a moment the imagery of Francis Bacon, Lord Verulam, he has learned how to effectuate in his own personality "a new birth in time," to wear a new body of desire, intention, and purpose; he has fitted to that body a new mind, and other objects of research. In fine, he has been taught how to lay it aside, and yet again he has been taught how to take it up after a different manner, in the midst of a very strange symbolism.

IMPERFECT SYMBOLISM

Now, it may be observed that in delineating these intimations of our symbolism, I seem already to have departed from the mystery of building with which I opened the conference; but I have been considering various sidelights thereon. It may be understood, further, that I am not claiming to deal with a symbolism that is perfect in all its parts, however honorable it may be otherwise to the builder. During such research as I have been enabled to make into the Instituted Mysteries of different ages and countries, I have never met with one which was in entire harmony with itself. We must be content with what we have, just as it is necessary to tolerate the peculiar conventions of language under which the Craft Degrees have passed into expression, artificial and sometimes commonplace as they are. Will you observe once again at this stage how it is only in the first Degree that the Candidate is instructed to build upon his own part a superstructure which is somehow himself? This symbolism is lost completely in the ceremony of the Fellowcraft Degree, which, roughly speaking, is something of a Degree of Life; the symbols being more especially those of conduct and purpose, while in the Third Degree, they speak of direct relations between man and his Creator, giving intimation of judgment to come.

THE THIRD DEGREE

I have said, and you know, that the Master's Degree is one of death and resurrection of a certain kind, and among its remarkable characteristics there is a return to building symbolism, but this time in the form of a legend. It is no longer an erection of the Candidate's own house — house of the body, house of the mind, and house of the moral law. We are taken to the Temple of Solomon and are told how the Master-Builder suffered martyrdom rather than betray the mysteries which had been placed in his keeping. Manifestly the lesson which is drawn in the Degree is a veil of something much deeper, and about which there is no real intimation. It is assuredly an instruction for the Candidates that they must keep the secrets of the Masonic Order, but such a covenant has reference only to the official and external side. The bare recitation of the legend would have been sufficient to enforce this; but observe that the Candidate assumes the part of the Master-Builder and suffers within or in him as a testimony of personal faith and honor in respect to his engagements. But thereafter he rises, and it is this which gives a peculiar characteristic to the descriptive title of the Degree. It is one of raising and of reunion with companions — almost as if he had been released from earthly life and had entered the true Land of the Living. The keynote is therefore not one of dying but one of resurrection; and yet it is not said in the legend that the Master rose. The point seems to me one of considerable importance, and yet I know not of a single place in our literature wherein it has received consideration. I will leave it, however, for the moment, but with the intention of returning to it.

PART II

There are two ways in which the Master's Degree may be thought to lapse from perfection in respect of its symbolism, and I have not taken out a license to represent it as of absolute order in these or in any respects. This has been practically intimated already. Perhaps it is by the necessity of things that it has recourse always to the lesser meaning, for it is this which is more readily understood. On the other hand, much must be credited to its subtlety, here and there, in the best sense of the term. There is something to be said for an allegory which he who runs may read, at least up to a certain point. But those who made the legend, and the ritual could not have been unaware of that which the deeper side shows forth; they have left us also the Opening and Closing as of the great of all greatness — so it seems to me, my Brethren — in things of ceremony and ritual. Both are devoid of explanation, and it is for us to understand them as we can.

For myself it is obvious that something distinct from the express motives of Masonry has come to us in this idea of Raising. The Instituted Mysteries of all ages and countries were concerned in the figuration, by means of ritual and symbolism, of New Birth, a new life, a mystic death, and resurrection, as so many successive experiences through which the Candidate passed on the way of his inward progress from earthly to spiritual life, or from darkness to light. The Ritual or Book of the Dead is a case in point. It has been for a long period regarded by scholarship as intimating the after-death experiences or adventures of the soul in the halls of judgment, and so forth; but there are traces already of the genesis of a new view, chiefly in the writing of Mr. W. Flinders Petrie, according to which some parts at least of this great text are really a rite of initiation and advancement, through which Candidates pass in this life.

THE BOOK OF THE DEAD

If I am putting this rather strongly as regards one important authority, it is at least true to say that he appears to discern the mystical side of the old Egyptian texts, while there are others, less illustrious than he, who have gone much further in this direction. It is very difficult for one like me, although unversed in Egyptology, to study such a work as Osiris and the Egyptian Resurrection, by E. Wallis Budge, without feeling very strongly that there is much to be said for this view, or without hoping that it will be carried further by those who are properly warranted.

So far as it is possible to speak of the Kabiric Mysteries, there was in those an episode of symbolical death, because Kasmillos, a technical name ascribed to the Candidate, was represented as slain by the gods. Some of the rites which prevailed within and around Greece in ancient times are concerned with the idea of a regeneration or new birth. The Mysteries of Bacchus depicted the death of this god and his restoration to light as Rhea. Osiris died and rose, and so also did Adonis. He was first lamented as dead and then his revivification was celebrated with great joy. There is no need, however, to multiply the recurrence of these events in the old Mysteries nor to restrict ourselves within their limits, for all religions have testified to the necessity of regeneration and have administered its imputed processes. That which is most important − from my point of view − is the testimony belonging to Christian times and the secret tradition therein.

THE CHRISTIAN MYSTERIES

Of course, to speak of this it is necessary to trend on subjects which at present are excluded, and very properly so, from discussion in a Craft Lodge, when they are presented from a religious and doctrinal angle. I shall not treat them from that standpoint, but rather as a sequence of symbolism in the form of dramatic mystery, alluding slightly, and from a philosophical point of view only, to the fact that in certain schools they are regarded as delineating momentous experiences in the history and life of man's soul. That new birth which conferred upon the *Eleusinian mystae* the title of Regenerated Children of the Moon − so that each one of them was henceforth symbolically a Son of the Queen of Heaven − born as a man originally and reborn in a divine manner − has its correspondence on a much higher plane of symbolism with the Divine Birth in Bethlehem, according to which a child was "born" and a son "given," who, in hypothesis at least, was the Son of God, but Son also of Mary — one of whose titles, according to Latin theology, is Queen of Heaven.

The hidden life in Egypt and Nazareth corresponds to the life of seclusion led by the *mystae* during their period of probation between the Lesser and Greater Mysteries. The three years of ministry are in analogy with the Temple-functions of the mystagogues. But lastly, in Egypt and elsewhere, there was the mystic experience of the Pastos, in which the initiate died symbolically, as Jesus died upon the Cross. The Christian "Symbolum" says: — *Descendit ad inferos*: that is, "He descended into hell"; and in the entranced condition of the Pastos, the soul of the Postulant was held or was caused to wander in certain spiritual realms. But in fine, it is said of Christ: — *Tertia die resurrexit*; "the third day he rose again from the dead." So also, the Adept of the Greater Mysteries rose from the Pastos in the imputed glory of an inward illumination.

THE MYSTICAL FACT

There was a period not so long ago when these analogies were recognized and applied to place a fabulous construction upon the central doctrines of Christian religion, just as there was a period when the solar mythology was adapted in the same direction. We have no call to consider these aberrations of a partially digested learning; but they had their excuses in their period. The point on which I would insist is that in the symbolism of the old initiations, and in the pageant of the Christian mythos, there is held to be the accurate delineation of a mystical experience, the heads, and sections of which correspond to the notions of mystic birth, life, death, and resurrection. It is a particular formula which is illustrated frequently in the mystic literature of the western world. Long before Symbolic Masonry had emerged above the horizon, several cryptic texts of alchemy, in my understanding, were bearing witness to this symbolism and to something real in experience which lay behind it. In more formal Christian mysticism, it was not until the 16th century and later that it entered the fullest expression.

Now, that which is formulated as mystic birth is comparable to a dawn of spiritual consciousness. It is the turning of the whole life-motive in the divine direction, so that, at a given time — which is actually the point of turning — the personality stands symbolically between the East and the North, between the greatest zone of darkness and that zone which is the source of light, looking towards the light-source and realizing that the whole nature has to be renewed therein. Mystic life is a quest for divine knowledge in a world that is within. It is the life led in this light, progressing and developing therein, as if a brother should read the Mysteries of Nature and Science with new eyes cast upon the record, which record is everywhere, but more especially in his own mind and heart. It is the complete surrender to the working of the divine, so that an hour comes when proprium *meum et tuum* dies in the mystical sense, because it is hidden in God. In this state, by the testimony of many literatures, there supervenes an experience which is described in a thousand ways yet remains ineffable. It has been enshrined in the imperishable books of Plato and Plotinus. It glimmers forth at every turn and corner of the remote roads and pathways of Eastern philosophies. It is in little books of unknown authorship, treasured in monasteries and most of which have not entered into knowledge, except within recent times.

THE PLACE OF DARKNESS

The experience is in a place of darkness, where, in other symbolism, the sun is said to shine at midnight. There is afterwards that further state, in which the soul of man returns into the normal physical estate, bringing the knowledge of another world, the quest ended for the time being at least. This is compared to resurrection, because in the aftermath of his experience the man is, as it were, a new being. I have found in most mythological legends that the period between divine death and resurrection was triadic and is spoken of roughly as three days, though there is an exception is the case of Osiris, whose dismemberment necessitated a long quest before the most important of his organs was left finally lost. The three days are usually foreshortened at both ends; the first is an evening, the second a complete day, while the third ends at sunrise. It is an allusion to the temporal brevity ascribed in all literatures to the culminating mystical experience. It is remarkable, in this connection, that during the mystic death of the Candidate in the Third Degree, the time of his interned condition is marked by three episodes, which are so many attempts to raise him, the last only being successful.

OPERATIVE MASONRY

Two things follow unquestionably from these considerations, so far as they have proceeded. The interest in Operative Masonry and its records, though historically it is of course important, has proceeded from the beginning on a misconception as to the aims and symbolism of Speculative Masonry. It was and it remains natural, and it has not been without its results, but it is a confusion of the chief issues. It should be recognized henceforward that the sole connection between the two Arts and Crafts rests on the fact that the one has undertaken to uplift the other from the material plane to that of morals on the surface and of spirituality in the real intention. Many things led up thereto, and a few of them were at work unconsciously within the limits of Operative Masonry. At a period when there was a tendency to symbolize everything roughly, so that it might receive a tincture of religion — I speak of the Middle Ages — the duty of Apprentice to Master, and of Master to pupil, had analogies with relations subsisting between man and God, and they were not lost sight of in those old Operative documents. Here was a rudiment capable of indefinite extension. The placing of the Lodges and of the Craft at large under notable patronage, and the subsequent custom of admitting persons of influence, offered another and quite distinct opportunity. These facts notwithstanding, my position is that the traces of symbolism which may in a sense be inherent in Operative Masonry did not produce, by a natural development, the Speculative Art and Craft, though they helped undoubtedly to make a possible and partially prepared field for the great adventure and experiment.

THE OLD CHARGES

The second point is that we must take the highest intention of symbolism in the Third Degree to some extent apart from the setting. You will know that the literary history of our ritual is non-existent rather than obscure, or if this is putting the case a little too strongly, it remains that researches have so far left the matter in a dubious position. The reason is not for our seeking, for the kind of enquiry that is involved is one of exceeding difficulty. If I say that it is my personal aspiration to undertake it one of these days, I speak of what is perhaps a distant hope. What is needed is a complete codification of all the old copies, in what language soever, which are scattered through the Lodges and libraries of the whole Masonic world, together with an approximate determination of their dates by expert evidence. In my opinion, the codices now in use have their roots in the 18th century but were edited and re-edited at an even later date.

I have now brought before you in somewhat disjointed manner — as I cannot help feeling — several independent considerations, each of which, taken separately, institutes certain points of correspondence between Masonry and other systems of symbolism, but they do not at present enter into harmony. I will collect them as follows: —

(1) Masonry has for its object, under one aspect, the building of the Candidate as a house or temple of life. Degrees outside the Craft aspire to this building as a living stone in a spiritual temple, meet for God's service.

(2) Masonry also presents a symbolical sequence, but in a somewhat crude manner, of Birth, Life, Death, and Resurrection, which other systems indicate as a mystery of experience.

(3) Masonry, in fine, represents the whole body of its *Adepti* as in search of something that has been lost, and it tells us how and with whom that loss came about.

These are separate and independent lines of symbolism, though, as indicated already, they are interlinked by the fact of their incorporation in Craft Masonry, considered as a unified system. But the truth is that between the spiritual building of the First Degree and the Legend of Solomon's Temple there is so little essential correspondence that one was never intended to lead up to the other. The symbolism of the Entered Apprentice Degree is of the simplest and most obvious kind; it is also personal and individualistic.

That of the Master's Degree is complex and remote in its significance; it is, moreover, an universal mythos. I have met with some searchers of the mysteries who seem prepared to call it cosmic, but I must not carry you so far as this speculation would lead us, and I do not hold a brief for its defense. I am satisfied in my own mind that the Third Degree has been grafted on the others and does not belong to them. There has been no real attempt to weld them, but they have been drawn into some kind of working sequence by the Exhortation which the Worshipful Master recites prior to the dramatic scene in the last Master's Degree. To these must be added some remarks to the Candidate immediately after the Raising. The Legend is reduced therein to the uttermost extent possible in respect of its meaning, though it is possible that this has been done of set purpose.

LIVING STONES

It will be seen that the three aspects enumerated above fall under two heads in their final analysis, the first representing a series of practical counsels, thinly allegorized upon in terms of symbolic architecture. The Candidate is instructed to work towards his own perfection under the light of Masonry. There is no mystery, no concealment whatever, and it calls for no research in respect of its source. Its analogies and replicas are everywhere, especially in religious systems. It reflects the Pauline doctrine that man is or may become a temple of the Holy Spirit. But it should be observed in this connection that there is a rather important-though confusing mixture of images in the address of the Worshipful Master to the Candidate, after the latter has been invested and brought to the East. It is pointed out to him that he represents the cornerstone of a building — as it might be, the whole Masonic edifice but he is immediately counselled to raise a superstructure from the foundation of that cornerstone — thus reversing the image. That of the cornerstone is like an externalization in dramatic form of an old Rosicrucian maxim belonging to the year 1629: — "Be ye transmuted from dead stones into living, philosophical stones."

From my point of view, it is the more important side of the symbolism; it is as if the great Masonic edifice were to be raised on each Candidate; and if every Neophyte shaped his future course both in and out of Masonry, as though this were the case actually, I feel that the Royal Art would be other than it now is and that our individual lives would differ.

PART III

Recurring to the Legend of the Third Degree, the pivot upon which it revolves is the existence of a building secret, represented as a Master-Word, which the Builder died to preserve. Owing to his untimely death, the Word was lost, and it has always been recognized in Masonry that the Temple, unfinished at the moment of the untoward event, remained with its operations suspended and was completed later on by those who obviously did not possess the Word or key. The tradition has descended to us and, as I have said, we are still on the quest.

Now what does all this mean? We have no concern at the present day, except in archaeology and history, with King Solomon's Temple. What is meant by this Temple and what is the Lost Word? These things have a meaning, or our system is stultified. Well, here are burning questions, and the only direction in which we can look for an answer is their source. As to this, we must remember that the Legend of the Master's Degree is a Legend of Israel, under the aegis of the Old Covenant, and though it has no warrants in the Holy Writ which constitutes the Old Testament, it is not antecedently improbable that something to our purpose may be found elsewhere in the literature of Jewry.

The Kabalah

I do not of course mean that we shall meet with the Legend itself; it would be interesting if we did but not per se helpful, apart from explanation. I believe in my heart that I have found what is much more important, and this is the root-matter of that which is shadowed forth in the Legend, as regards the meaning of the Temple and the search for the Lost Word. There are certain great texts which are known to scholars under the generic name of Kabalah, a Hebrew word meaning reception, or doctrinal teaching passed on from one to another by verbal communication. According to its own hypothesis, it entered into written records during the Christian era, but hostile criticism has been disposed to represent it as invented at the period when it was written. The question does not signify for our purpose, as the closing of the 13th century is the latest date that the most drastic view — now generally abandoned — has proposed for the most important text.

We find therein after what manner, according to mystic Israel, Solomon's Temple was spiritualized; we find deep meanings attached to the two pillars *J.* and *B.*; we find how the word was lost and under what circumstances the chosen people were to look for its recovery. It is an expectation for Jewish theosophy, as it is for the Craft Mason. It was lost owing to an untoward event, and although the time and circumstances of its recovery have been calculated in certain texts of the Kabalah, there has been something wrong with the methods. The keepers of the tradition died with their faces toward Jerusalem, looking for that time; but for Jewry at large the question has passed from the field of view, much as the quest is continued by us in virtue of a ceremonial formula but cannot be said to mean anything for those who undertake and pursue it. It was lost owing to the unworthiness of Israel, and the destruction of the First Temple was one consequence thereof. By the waters of

Babylon, in their exile, the Jews are said to have remembered Zion, but the word did not come back into their hearts; and when Divine Providence inspired Cyrus to bring about the building of the Second Temple and the return of Israel into their own land, they went back empty of all recollection in this respect.

THE DIVINE NAME

I am putting things in a summary fashion that are scattered up and down the vast text with which I am dealing — that is to say, *Sepher Ha Zohar, The Book of Splendor*. The word to which reference is made is the Divine Name out of the consonants of which, *He, Vau, He, Yod*, we have formed Jehovah, or more accurately Yahve. When Israel fell into a state which is termed impenitence it is said in the Zoharic Symbolism that the *Vau* and the *He* final were separated. The name was dismembered, and this is the first sense of loss which is registered concerning it. The second is that it has no proper vowel points, those of the Name Elohim being substituted, or alternatively the Name *Adonai*. It is said, for example: "My Name is written *YHVH* and read *Adonai*." The epoch of restoration and completion is called, almost indifferently, that of resurrection, the world to come, and the advent of the Messiah. In such day the present imperfect separation between the letters will be put an end to, once and forever. If it be asked: What is the connection between the loss and dismemberment which befell the Divine Name *Jehovah* and the *Lost Word in Masonry*, I cannot answer too plainly; but every Royal Arch Mason knows that which is communicated to him in that Supreme Degree, and in the light of the present explanation he will see that the "great" and "incomprehensible" thing so imparted comes to him from the Secret Tradition of Israel.

It is also to this Kabalistic source, rather than to the variant accounts in the first book of Kings and in Chronicles, that we must have recourse for the important Masonic Symbolism concerning the Pillars J. and B. There is very little in Holy Scripture which would justify a choice of these objects as representatives of our art of building spiritualized.

But in later Kabalism, in the texts called "The Garden of Pomegranates" and in "The Gates of Light," there is a very full and complicated explanation of the strength which is attributed to B., the left-hand Pillar, and of that which is established in and by the right-hand Pillar, called J.

THE TEMPLE

As regards the Temple itself, I have explained at length elsewhere after what manner it is spiritualized in various Kabalistic and semi-Kabalistic texts, so that it appears ever as "the proportion of the height, the proportion of the depth, and the lateral proportions" of the created universe, and again as a part of the transcendental mystery of law which is at the root of the secret tradition in Israel. This is outside our subject, not indeed in its nature but owing to the limitations of opportunity. I will say only that it offers another aspect of a fatal loss in Israel and the world — which is commented on in the tradition. That which the Temple symbolized above all things was, however, a House of Doctrine, and as on the one hand the Zohar shows us how a loss and substitution were perpetuated through centuries, owing to the idolatry of Israel at the foot of Mount Horeb in the wilderness of Sinai, and illustrated by the breaking of the Tables of Stone on which the Law was inscribed; so does Speculative Masonry intimate that the Holy House, which was planned and begun after one manner, was completed after another and a word of death was substituted for a word of life.

The Builder

I shall not need to tell you that beneath such veils of allegory and amidst such illustrations of symbolism, the Master-Builder signifies a principle and not a person, historical or otherwise. He signifies indeed more than a single principle, for in the world of mystic intimations through which we are now moving, the question, "Who is the Master?" would be answered by many voices. But generically, he is the imputed life of the Secret- Doctrine which lays beyond the letter of the Written Law, which "the stiff-necked and disobedient" of the patriarchal, sacerdotal and prophetical dispensations contrived to destroy. According to the Secret Tradition of Israel, the whole creation was established for the manifestation of this life, which became manifested in its dual aspect when the spiritual Eve was drawn from the side of the spiritual Adam and placed over against him, in the condition of face to face. The intent of creation was made void in the event, which is called the Fall of Man, though the expression is unknown in Scripture. By the hypothesis, the "fatal consequences" which followed would have reached their time on Mount Sinai, but the Israelites, when left to themselves in the wilderness, "sat down to eat and rose up to play." That which is concealed in the evasion of the last words corresponds the state of Eve in Paradise when she had become affected by the serpent.

To sum up as regards the sources, the Lost Word in Masonry is derived from a Kabalistic thesis of imperfection in the Divine Name *Jehovah*, by which the true pronunciation — that is to say, the true meaning — is lost. It was the life of the House of Doctrine, represented by the Temple planned of old in Israel. The Master-Builder is the Spirit, Secret or Life of the Doctrine; and it is the quest of this that every Mason takes upon himself in the ceremony of the Third Degree, so that the House, which in the words of another Masonic Degree, is now, for want of territory, built only in the heart, "a superstructure perfect in its parts and honorable to the builder."

CRAFT MASONRY

But if these are the sources of Craft Masonry, taken at its culmination in the Sublime Degree, what manner of people were those who grafted so strange a speculation and symbolism on the Operative procedure of a building Guild? The answer is that all about that period which represents what is called the transition, or during the 16th and 17th centuries, the Latin writing scholars were animated with zeal for the exposition of the tradition in Israel, with the result that many memorable and even great books were produced on the subject. Among those scholars were many great names, and they provided the materials ready for the hands of the symbolists. What was the purpose of the latter view? The answer is that in Germany, Italy, France and England, the Zeal for Kabalistic literature among the Latin-writing scholars had not merely a scholastic basis. They believed that the texts of the Secret Tradition showed plainly, out of the mouth of Israel itself, that the Messiah had come. This is the first fact. The second I have mentioned already, namely, that although the central event of the Third Degree is the Candidate's Raising, it is not said in the Legend that the Master-Builder rose, thus suggesting that something remains to come after, which might at once complete the legend and conclude the quest. The third fact is that in a rather early and important High Degree of the philosophical kind, now almost unknown, the Master-Builder of the Third Degree rises as Christ, and so completes the dismembered Divine Name, by insertion of the Hebrew letter Shin, this producing *Yeheshua* — the restoration of the Lost Word in the Christian Degrees of Masonry.

Of course, I am putting this point only as a question of fact in the development of symbolism. Meanwhile, I trust that, amidst many imperfections, I have done something to indicate a new ground for our consideration, and to show that the speaking mystery of the Opening and Closing of the Third Degree and the Legend of the Master-Builder come from what may seem to us very far away, but yet not so distant that it is impossible to trace them to their source.

Emblematic Freemasonry, Building Guilds, and Hermetic Schools

As EMBLEMATIC FREEMASONRY is the Craft of Building moralized, it follows that intellectually, at least, our figurative and speculative art has arisen out of the Operative. Here is a first link in any chain of connection with the building world of the past. But it seems certain also that the Free and Accepted, or Speculative, Masons had Operative documents, such as the so-called Gothic Constitutions and Old Charges, for part of their heritage. The proof is that soon after the revival of 1717, these documents were put into the hands of Dr. James Anderson "to digest ... in a new and better method." They were things apparently in evidence, and he was not commissioned to search them out. Beyond this omnia exeunt in *mysterium*. Almost year to year our documentary knowledge of Constitutions, Charges, and Landmarks extends slowly. There is also new light cast from time to time on the general history of architecture in Christian times. But no light is shed on the antiquities of art of building moralized. The existence of such an art prior to 1717 remains almost as much a matter of speculation as the art itself is speculative. We are led almost irresistibly to infer that it anteceded this date, and a few remain among us who believe that it may have been old in the year 1646, when Ashmole was made a Mason at Warrington, but there is no real evidence. So, also, there are zealous and capable writers by whom our knowledge is expanded from time to time, however slightly, on particular sides and respecting the archaeology of architectural history, on Roman Collegia, Dionysian artificers, and Comacines. They furnish at the same time many plausible and taking speculations. But they do not help us in respect of Freemasonry, as we now understand the term, because no evidence of building association is of service to our awn purpose unless such association embodies our "peculiar system of morality, veiled in allegory and illustrated by symbols."

The Hittites of Syria and Asia Minor may have been of "Hametic descent" and may have built the Temple at Jerusalem; the Etruscans, from whom architecture was learned by the Romans, may have been Hittites; at the downfall of Rome, the Roman Collegia may have settled in that island on Lake Como, which is familiar at the present day as *Isola Cpmacina*, and may have become Comacines; the Comacines may, in turn, have merged into the great Masonic guilds of the Middle Ages. But, if so, all this is part and parcel of the history of architecture and not of Emblematical Building, unless and until we can show that, practical Masons as they were, their system of secret association included what is called in the Craft degrees a side of Speculative Masonry and in the appendant degrees an art of building spiritualized. But it is just this which is wanting, or we should have taken the closing long since in the lodge of our debate on the origin of Freemasonry. There are not unnatural sporadic vestiges, few and far between. It is said that the Comacines had a motto affirming that their temple was "one made without hands," and this reminds us assuredly of the Mark degree; but it is not to be called evidence for a developed speculative element prevailing amongst those old masters. Nor can I think with Brother Ravenscroft, in his memorable series of papers contributed to *The Builder* in 1918, that the two pillars of Wurzburg Cathedral, once situated on either side of the porch and bearing respectively on their capitals the letters J and B, can be termed "a good illustration of the way in which symbols were transmitted even from the temple of Solomon to the medieval craftsmen and thence to our Speculative Masonry." It seems to me simply that the Cathedral builders were acquainted with Holy Scripture.

The conclusion which is forced upon me is that only using liberal supposition can the Comacines and those who preceded them be made to connect with our subject. We may take H.J. Da Costa as an early authority in England for the Dionysian fraternity and his successor, Krause, for the links between Masons of the Middle Ages and the Roman Collegia. The views of both have been summarized ably by my friend, Brother Joseph Fort Newton, but that which is valid therein belongs to the history of architecture. It was, I think, Krause who said that each Roman collegium was presided over by a Master and two *decuriones* or Wardens, each of whom bore the Master's commands to the brethren of his respective column. The word "decurio" is here translated "warden," to institute an analogy by force. According to Suetonius, the Latin office in question was that of a captain over ten men, whether horse or foot, and was therefore military in character. The first authority on the Comacines is Leader Scott (who is Miss Lucy E. Baxter) in "The Cathedral Builders," a most fascinating romance of architecture, which also contains some great and valuable historical lights. Joseph Fort Newton described it as an attempt to bridge the gap "between the classical Roman side and the rise of Gothic art." Again, therefore, it is a question of architectural evolution, and I must personally say that, taken as such, it is to be questioned whether the gulf is really spanned. I can understand on the hypothesis the development of Italian architecture, degenerated from classical types, but not the genesis of the great schools of Gothic building. It is to be understood, however, that this question exceeds the warrants of my subject to connect any ritual mystery which obtained *ex hypothesi* in the old Collegia, or among Comacine lodges, with the living mystery of Speculative Masonry, of which she speaks with derision, but evidently knows it only through an Italian source. As a student of the Secret Tradition in Christian times I could wish that the facts were otherwise in the great story of all these ancient guilds. I could have wished that their supposed

31

pageants of secret initiation were, as the speculations say, Dionysian representations of mystical death and erection, and that they are reflected at a far distance in our Sublime degree. But if these stories are dreams, or still awaiting demonstration, we must face the fact, and the question remaining over is whether we can look elsewhere. Now, it happens that there is one direction which has been regarded unfavorably as a possible source of light. It is that of Hermetic Schools in England, and these, speaking broadly, may be classified into three — Alchemical, Rosicrucian, and Kabalistic. They had a common bond of interest and tended here, as elsewhere, to merge one into another. There is evidence to show that the experiment of Alchemy in England is an exceedingly old pursuit, but in the early part of the seventeenth century it had sprung into greater prominence. The rumor of the Rosicrucian fraternity was also raising curiosity in Europe. Hermetic literature — not only with a modern accent but also for the time in vernacular language — extended greatly, and schools of theosophy sprang up in several countries. The root of the Rosicrucian movement was in Germany, but the impulse reached England and some of the most famous names connected with the subject are identified with this country. Hence came Alexander Seton and hence Eirenaeus Philalethes, who has been regarded as one of the great masters of Hermetic Art. Here also was Robert Fludd, who must, I think, be regarded as not only advocate and apologist in chief of the Rosicrucian art and philosophy, but as a fountain-head. Here, too, was Thomas Vaughan, mystic as well as alchemist. And here, in 1640, lived Elias Ashmole, alchemist and antiquary, founder also of the Ashmolean Museum at Oxford.

A section of Masonic opinion has looked in the past and a section looks still towards Elias Ashmole and his connections in some way, yet undetermined, as the representatives of this transition from Operative to Speculative Masonry. In France there has been practically no doubt on the subject from the days of Ragon, though concerning the value of his personal view I must speak with desirable plainness elsewhere in this paper. In America the distinguished name of Albert Pike can be cited in support of the thesis. After every allowance has been made for the position of such a speculation, still almost inextricable, it can be affirmed that it seems to offer a place of repose for all the tolerable views, because it does harmonize all — on the understanding that Ashmole and his consociates are not regarded personally but as typifying a leavening spirit introduced there and here, and at work during the period intervening between 1640 and the foundation of the first Grand Lodge in 1717. Pike was like Ragon unfortunately, a man of uncritical mind, and summarize his findings under all needful reserve.

Among Masonic symbols which he identifies used in common by Freemasons and Hermetic and Alchemical literature are the Square and Compasses, the Triangle, the Oblong Square, the legend of the three Grand Masters, the idea embodied in a substitute word, which might well be the most important of all together with the Sun, the Moon, and Master of the lodge. It was, moreover, his opinion, based on this and other considerations, that the philosophers — meaning the members of the Hermetic confraternities — became Freemasons and introduced into Masonry their own symbolism. He thinks finally that Ashmole was led to be made a Mason because others who were followers of Hermes had taken the step before him. However this may be, I have said elsewhere that the influence of the Rosicrucian fraternity upon that of Masons has been questioned only by those who by those who have been unfitted to appreciate the symbolism which they possess in common. It does not belong to the formative period of Emblematic Freemasonry, but to that of development and expansion. The nature of the influence is another matter and one, moreover, in which it may be necessary to recognize the simple principle of imitation up to a certain point. The influence has been exercised more especially in connection with other Rites, as to which it is impossible, for example, to question that those who instituted the eighteenth degree of the Scottish Rite either must have received something by transmission from the old German Brotherhood, or, alternatively, must have borrowed from its literature.

That Ashmole was connected with Rosicrucian, or otherwise with the representatives of some association which had assumed their name, is an inference drawn from his life. His antiquarian studies led him more especially in the direction of Alchemy but regards this art he did not remain an antiquary or a mere collector of old documents on the subject. He was, to some extent, a practical student and, moreover, not simply an isolated inquirer. He had secured the assistance which has been regarded always as essential, next only to the instruction of a Master. The alternative is Divine Aid, which is, of course, a higher kind of Mastery. He was associated otherwise with many of the occult philosophers, alchemist astrologers, and so forth, belonging to his period. The suggestion that he acted as an instrument of the Rosicrucian Brotherhood, or as a member thereof, in transfiguration of Operative into Speculative Freemasonry is a matter of faith for those who have held hold it. Of direct or indirect evidence there is no particle. Supposing that such a design existed at period, he is not an unlikely person to have been concerned in planning it on the part of himself and others or to have been delegated for such a purpose. But the design there is again no evidence. It has been affirmed further in the interests of the claim that meeting of an Alchemical – presumably Rosicrucian – society perceiving how working Masons were already outnumbered in membership by persons of education not belonging to the trade, believed that the time was ripe for a complete ceremonial revolution and that one founded on mystic tradition was drawn up thereon in writing, constituting the Entered Apprentice grade, approximately as it exists now. The grade of Fellow Craft was elaborated in 1648, and that of Master Mason in 1659.

These are the reveries of Ragon, categorical in nature, accompanied by specific details, all in the absence of one particle of fact in any record of the past. It seems to me, therefore, that no language would be too strong to characterize such mendacities and that they can belong only to the class of conscious lying, but the charge against Ragon is more especially that he elaborated the materials of a hypothesis which had grown up among successive inventors belonging to the type of Reghellini. If there were Rosicrucians in England at the date in question, it may be presumed that those who, according to Ashmole's own statement, communicated to him some portions, at least, of the Hermetic secrets would not have withheld the corporate mysteries of their Fraternity. But, on the other hand, there is at present no historical certainty that the Hermetic Order possessed any such corporate existence in England at that period. However this may be, in the memoirs of the life of Elias Ashmole, as drawn up by himself in the form of a diary, there is the following now well-known entry under date of 16th October, 1646:

I was made a Freemason at Warrington in Lancashire with Colonel Henry Mainwaring of Kartichan in Cheshire; the names of those that were then at the Lodge: Mr. Richard Penket, Warden; Mr. James Collier, Mr. Richard Sankey, Henry Littler, John Ellam, Richard Ellam, and Hugh Brewer.

The two noteworthy points in this extract, over and above the main fact which it designs to place on record, are that neither candidate was an operative by business and that the work of initiation was performed evidently by the brother who acted as Warden. At that period Elias Ashmole was under thirty years of age. His father was a saddler by trade, his mother was the daughter of a draper and he himself solicited in Chancery. But while still in his youth he tells us that he had entered that condition to which he had always aspired, "that I might be able to live to myself and studies, without being forced to take pains for a livelihood in the world." The admissions of 16th October 1646, are not required to prove the practice of initiating men of other business than that of Masonry and its connected crafts, or even of no business at all, but it should be observed that here — as in cases of earlier date — the reception was in the capacity of simple brothers and not of patrons.

The nature of those studies which were engrossing Ashmole about the time of his initiation may be learned by the publication, five years later, of his *Theatrum Chemicum Britannicum*, being a collection of metrical treatises written in English at various dates on the subject of the Hermetic Mystery and the Philosopher's Stone. They appear to be connected only with what is technically called the physical work on metals and physical medicine or elixir, not with those spiritual mysteries which have passed occasionally into expression under the peculiar symbolism of Alchemy. At the same time Ashmole is careful to explain his personal assurance that the transmutation of metals is only one branch of Hermetic practice:

> As this is but a part, so it is the least share of that blessing which may be acquired by the Philosopher's *materia*, if the full virtue thereof were known. Gold, I confess, is a delicious object, a goodly light which we admire and gaze upon *ut pueri in Junonis avem*, but as to make gold is the chief intent of the Alchemists, so was it scarcely any intent of the ancient Philosophers and the lowest use the Adeptio made of this *materia*. For they, being lovers of wisdom more than worldly

wealth, drove at higher and more excellent operations; and certainly he to whom the whole course of Nature lies open rejoiceth not so much that he can make gold and silver or the devils be made subject to him as that he sees the heavens open, the angels of God ascending and descending and that his own name is fairly written in the *Book of Life*.

It should be added that this exposition is a faithful reflection of Rosicrucian doctrine as it is put forward, directly or indirectly, under the name of the Brotherhood in German books and pamphlets of the seventeenth century. Supposing that circa 1650 there, was an incorporated Rosicrucian School in England, no person is so likely to have been a member as Ashmole, and it is not possible to imagine him in separation therefrom. Indeed, I am by no means certain that his testimony is not thinly presumptive of membership, being so to the manner born of it in thought and figures of speech. But if we can tolerate — however tentatively — the Rosicrucian initiation of Ashmole, we may take it for granted that he did not stand alone. Overall, it seems barely possible that on 16th October 1646, a brother of the Rosy Cross was made a Mason, with or without an ulterior motive in view. It follows expressly from his frank and honorable testimony concerning himself that he was one who had only seen the end of adeptship, even within the measures that he conceived it, while as regards any other Rosicrucians to whom he may have been joined we know very little concerning them.

It will be seen that the Ashmole hypothesis is but a part of the wider claim of direct Rosicrucian influence on the foundation of Emblematic Freemasonry. I agree with the opinion that in so far as it has been advanced in the past this claim has lapsed. It affirms that the House of the Holy Spirit, being the Rosicrucian Brotherhood in Germany, had a Secret House in England, which either transfigured itself into the thing called Speculative Masonry or revolutionized the old Operative Craft along speculative lines for its own purposes, presumably that it might have recruiting centers available and more or less openly manifest. There is no evidence whatever to support this view. The Rosicrucian zeal of the occult philosopher and intellectual mystic, Robert Fludd, left no trace behind it, until the time came for it to influence in a rather indefinite manner the enthusiasm of Thomas Vaughan, and this also led to nothing. Rosicrucian Society in England of which we hear belongs to the early nineteenth century. In particular, Fludd's activities had no bearing on any Masonry of the early seventeenth century, even if Robertus de Fluctitus was the Mr. Flood who presented a *Book of Constitutions* to the Masons' Company, as recorded in an inventory taken before the Fire of London.

When the question at issue has been relieved from these reveries there remains the more reasonable suggestion that the Operative Brotherhood came gradually and not unnaturally under the influence of persons who belonged to both associations. It would also attract those who were simply Hermetic students, though isolated and unattached as such. Attached or otherwise, Ashmole is a case in point, though his place in Freemasonry of the mid-seventeenth century is a subject for very careful adjudication. The influence which in this manner would begin to be exercised, consciously or unconsciously, would be Hermetic in a general sense rather than Rosicrucian exclusively; but this is a distinction which will not be realized readily by those who are acquainted only at second-hand with the mystical and occult movements of the seventeenth century. As to the ritual side of the Operative Masonry in that century we know next to nothing, while of Rosicrucian ritual procedure—if any—we know nothing at all.

Such in rough outline is the case as it stands for the interference of two Hermetic Schools in Freemasonry prior to the first historical evidence for the ritual of the Third Craft degree and apart from any long since exploded hypothesis which has sought to connect the Brotherhood with older Mysteries by means of direct transmission within their own bonds. I have registered my feelings that someday it may assume a less uncertain aspect, in other words that sources of additional knowledge may become available. I know that the root-matter of the Third degree belongs to the Secret Tradition and is not only of the Hermetic Schools but of Schools thereunto antecedent. This is not a speculative question or one of simple persuasion. It is, moreover, no question of history and does not stand or fall with particular personalities and with claims made concerning them. As regards these, there is work remaining to be done — that is to say, in the purely historic field, but unfortunately the subject has only a few sympathizers in England and among these a small proportion only who are qualified to work therein. In the meantime, it remains that the position of Hermetic Schools, so far delineated, is not unlike that of speculation on Comacines, Roman Collegia, and Dionysian architects. When we pass, however, to the third Hermetic School the position is, I think, different. The root-matter of much that is shadowed forth in the traditional history of the Craft, as regards the meaning of the Temple and the search for the Lost Word, is to be found in certain great texts known to scholars under the generic name of Kabalah. We find therein after what manner, according to mystic Israel, Solomon's Temple was spiritualized — we find profound meanings attached to the two pillars *J* and *B*; we find how a Word was lost and under what circumstances the chosen people were to look for its recovery. It is expectation for Jewish theosophy, as it is for the Craft Mason. It was lost owing to a certain untoward event and although the time and circumstances of its recovery have been calculated in certain texts, there has been something amiss with the methods. Those who were keepers of the tradition died with their face towards Jerusalem, looking for that time; but Jewry at large the question has passed long since from the field of view, much as the quest is continued by Masons in virtue of a ceremonial formula but cannot be said to mean anything for those who undertake and pursue it officially. It was lost owing to the unworthiness of Israel, and the destruction of the First Temple was one consequence thereof. By the waters of Babylon, in their exile, the Jews are said to have remembered Zion, but the Word did not return into their hearts; and when Divine Providence inspired Cyrus to project the building of a second temple and the return of Israel into their own land, they went back empty of all recollection in this respect.

The Word to which reference is made in that Divine Name out of the consonants of which we have formed Jehovah, or, by another speculation, Yahve. When Israel fell into a state that is termed impenitence it is said in Zoharic symbolism that VAV and HE final were separated. The name was thus dismembered, and this is the first sense of loss which is registered concerning it. The second is that it has no proper vowel points, those of the name *ELOHIM* being substituted or alternatively, of the name *ADONAI*. It is said, for example: "My name is written *YHVH* and read *ADONAI*." The epoch of restoration and completion is called, almost indifferently, that of resurrection, the world to come and the advent of Messiah. In such day the present separation between the letters will reach its term, once and forever. It is also to this Kabalistic source, rather than the variant account in the first book of Kings or Chronicles, that we must have recourse for the important Masonic symbolism concerning the pillars *J* and *B*. There is very little in Holy Scripture to justify a choice of those objects as representatives of an art of building spiritualized. But in late Kabalism, in the texts called *The Garden of Pomegranates* and *The*

Gates of Light there is a very full planation of the strength, which is attributed to *B*, the left-hand pillar, and of that which is "established" in and by the right-hand pillar, called *J*. As regards the temple itself, I have explained elsewhere after what manner it is spiritualized in various Kabalistic and semi-Kabalistic texts, so that it appears as "the proportion of the height, the proportion of the depth, and the lateral proportion" of the created universe. It offers another aspect of the fatal loss Israel and the world which is commented on in the Tradition. That which the temple symbolizes above all things is, however, a House of Doctrine, and as the one hand the Zohar shows us how a loss and substitution were perpetuated through centuries, owing to the idolatry of Israel at the foot of Mount Horeb in the wilderness of Sinai, and illustrated by the breaking of the tables of stone on which the Law was inscribed, so, does Speculative Masonry intimate that the Holy House, which was planned and begun after one manner, was completed after another and a word of death was, substituted for a word of life.

But if these are among the sources of Craft Masonry, taken at its culmination in the Sublime degree, what manner of people were those who grafted so strange a speculation and symbolism on the Operative procedure of a building guild, even when this has been symbolized? The answer is that all about the period which represents what is called the "transition," and indeed between the sixteenth and eighteenth centuries many Latin-writing scholars of Europe were animated with zeal for an exposition of the tradition in Israel, with the result that memorable and even great books were produced on the subject. But this zeal for Kabalistic literature had more than a scholastic basis. It was believed that the texts of the Secret Tradition showed plainly, out of the mouth of Israel itself, that the Messiah had come. This is the first fact. The second is in Ceremonial Masonry itself, and, namely, that although the central event of the Third degree is the candidate's raising, it is not said in the legend that the Master Builder rose, thus suggesting that something remains to come after, which might at once complete the legend and conclude the quest. The third fact is that in an important high grade of a philosophical kind, now almost unknown, the Master Builder of the Third degree rises as Christ. The dismembered Divine Name is completed therein by insertion of the Hebrew letter *SHIN*, thus producing *YEHESHUAH*, the official restoration of the Lost Word in the Christian degrees of Masonry. It follows that although the opening and closing of the Third degree and the legend of the Master-Builder, with all their speaking Mysteries, may seem to come from very far away, they are not so remote that we cannot trace them to their source.

It is to be observed that the presence of a Kabalistic element in the traditional history of the Craft by no means connotes antiquity, and antiquity is a difficult thing, to predicate of the Third degree, at least in its present form. By whomsoever created or developed, its author was a student of the Secret Tradition in Israel, and drew great lights therefrom, possibly at first hand, but more probably perhaps from those Latin commentaries and synopses already mentioned. The bulk of these were already compiled, whether we place his work late in the seventeenth or early in the eighteenth century. Much of it was available previously, supposing that more considerable antiquity could be predicated of the Third degree. But we must cleave to that which is evidentially reasonable in this respect until time or circumstances shall provide better warrants. For Speculative Masonry as a whole we may have to rest content also, if we cannot date it much further back than the close of the seventeenth century, recognizing that its present characteristic developments are to be sought in and about the Revival period. Such recognition puts an end to romantic hypothesis, but the great intimations of the Third degree remain a speaking pageant in Symbolism, however late its origin. The quest of the

Word remains, with all Zoharic Theosophy behind it and all the rites of Christian Masonry in front. The mythos connects our Order with the figurative Mysteries of past ages, while the opening and closing of the lodge in that degree are much greater than anything in the memorials of Greece and Egypt.

I shall, therefore, reach a general conclusion on the Hermetic Schools and their alleged intervention for the transformation of an Operative Guild into an Emblematic Freemasonry and it shall be expressed in such a manner as will be without detriment to ourselves or our connections as loyal and devoted Masons. In Dionysian architects, Roman Collegia, Comacines, and Building Guilds of the Middle Ages, I have failed to discover any traces of an art of building spiritualized. I have taken the old Gothic Constitutions and have sought to digest them like Anderson "in a new and better method"; but however they were passed and repassed through the mental alembic, they have yielded nothing corresponding to a "system of morality veiled in allegory and illustrated by symbols." Not even the *Regius MSS.* betrays a single vestige, though I have followed Gould anxiously. As regards the Hermetic Schools, and speaking, if I may venture to say so, as one who knows the literature, the allegation of Albert Pike is true in respect of a few world-wide symbols which prove nothing and false in all things else. There is no legend of the three Grand Masters in Alchemy; there is no Substituted Word; and there is no Master of the lodge, for there is no need of ritual procedure among all its cloud of witnesses. The witness of Alchemy to Masonry is the witness of Elias Ashmole, the sole alchemist in the seventeenth century whom we know to have become a Mason. The Rosicrucian influence I believe to have been marked in character and exercised for a considerable period, but we know it only in its developments which belong to the eighteenth century, and are, of course, beyond our scope. Provisionally, and under all reserve, I am inclined to hold that it began earlier, but more especially as an atmosphere belonging to the formative period of Emblematic Freemasonry. But the great Rosicrucian maxim cited by Robert Fludd about 1630 must be ruled out. *Transmutemini, transmutemini de lapidibus mortuis in lapides vivos philosophicos*, does not signify that the brothers of the Rosy Cross had either joined or invented our figurative and speculative art; it is rather a contract established between material and spiritual alchemy. For the present, at least, we are asked also to set aside the winning speculation concerning a secret school of Emblematic Masonry co-existent through several generations or centuries with the Operative Guild and sometimes identified with Rosicrucians. There are no Rosicrucian traces prior to 1578. Moreover, the alleged school is a notion arising out of a false construction of the *Regius MS*.

We are left in this manner with the Kabalistic element about which I have spoken plainly. But now, as a last point, supposing that there is no trace of the Third degree prior to 1717, that after this epoch it was devised by a group of Masonic literate or alternatively by an anonymous brother, whether famous like Desaguliers, or obscure; what, then, is our position? My own at least is this: that the Third degree was formulated on the basis of the Ancient Mysteries and illustrated by the light of Kabalism: facts about which there is no open question; that it belongs as such to an old and secret tradition, though not in respect of time; that it stands on its own symbolical value and that, in the words of Martines de Pasqually: We must needs be content with what we have. As a student of the past, again I could wish that it were otherwise; but in this, as in all else, the first consideration is truth. There are high grades of Masonry for which no one in his senses predicates antiquity, and yet they are great grades. They are even holy grades, which, from my point of view, carry on the work of the Craft towards something that stands for completion. I conclude, therefore, with an affirmation which I have made in other places, that antiquary per se is not a test of value. I can imagine a rite created at this day which would be much greater and more eloquent in symbolism than anything that we work and love under the name of Masonry. Yet, for what Masonic antiquity is, let us call it two hundred years, under all needful reserves, such an invention would not have the hallowed and beloved associations which have grown about our Emblematic Craft. Here is the matter of antiquity which really signifies: it is part of the life of the Order. And after all the fables and all the fond reveries, the false analogies, and mythical identifications with other and immemorial Mysteries, it is again the life which counts, the life of that great world-wide Masonic organism, in which we ourselves live and move and have our Masonic being.

The French Mystic and the Story of Modern Martinism

The Great Day of Saint-Martin

During the second half of the eighteenth century, it may be said without exaggeration that the intellectual, historical, and political center of all things was in the kingdom of France. The statement is obtained not only because of the great upheaval of revolution, which was to close the epoch, but because of the activities which were prepared thereto. I know not what gulfs disparate us from the scheme and order of things signified by the name of Voltaire, by Diderot and the Encyclopedists at large, or what are the points of contact between the human understanding at this day and that which was conceived by Condorcet in his memorable treatise. But about the import and consequence of their place and time I suppose that no one can question. The same land and the same period were the center also of occult activities and occult interests, which I mention at once because they belong to my subject, at least on the external side, since it happens quite often that where occultism is about on the surface there is mysticism somewhere behind. We may remember in this connection that a Christian mystical influence had been carried over in France from the last years of the seventeenth century through certain decades which followed: it was that of Port Royal, Fenelon, and Madame Guyon, owing something — almost unawares — to the Spanish school of Quietism, as this in its turn reflected, without being aware of the fact, from pre-Reformation sources.

As regards occult activities, if I say that their seeds were sown prior to 1750, it will be understood that I am speaking of developments which were characteristic in a particular manner of the years that followed thereon. Occultism is always in the world, and among the French people especially there has been always some disposition to be drawn in this direction. In the eighteenth century, however, the sources for the most part are not to be found in France. The persuasive illuminations of Swedenborg the deep searching's of Jacob Bohme into God, man and the universe, the combined theosophy and magic represented by earlier and later Kabalism, and a strange new sense of the Mysteries coming out from a sleep of the centuries with the advent of Symbolical Freemasonry these and some others with a root of general likeness were foreign in respect of their origins, but they found their homes in France. So also, were certain splendid historical adventurers who were traffickers in the occult sciences, as other merchants traded the wares of the normal commercial world. I refer, of course, to Saint-Germain and Cagliostro, but they are signal examples or types, for they did not stand alone. There were men with new gospels and revelations of all kinds; there were alchemists and magi in the byways, as well as on the public roads and in the King's palaces. Perhaps above all there were those who were traffickers in Rites, meaning Masonic Rites, carrying strange charters, and making claims which had never been heard of previously in the age-long chronicle of occult things.

When one comes to reflect upon it, the great, many-sided Masonic adventure may be said to stand for the whole, to express it in the world of signs, as actually and historically speaking there came a day, before the French Revolution, when it seemed about to absorb the whole. All the occult sciences, all the ready-made evangels, all philosophies, the ever-transpiring new births in time ceased to be schemes on paper and came to be embodied in Grades.

So also, the past, though it may be thought to have buried its dead, began to give them back to the Rites, and not as sheeted ghosts, but as things so truly risen and so much affirming life that they denied their own death and even that they had fallen asleep. Of such was the Rosy Cross. It came about in this manner that our Emblematical Institution, which was born, so to speak, at an Apple-Tree Tavern and nursed in its early days at the Rummer and Grapes or the Goose and Gridiron, may be said to have passed through a second birth in France. It underwent otherwise a great transformation, was clothed in gorgeous vestments, and decorated with magnificent titles. It contracted in like manner the adornment of innumerable spiritual marriages, which were fruitful in spiritual progeny. I have pronounced its upcoming elsewhere and that of the Rites and Grades, the memorable Orders and Chivalries which came thus into being. More numerous still were the foster sons and daughters, being things connected with Masonry but not belonging thereto, even in the widest sense of its Emblematic Art. Of illegitimate children by scores, things of rank imposture or gross delusion, I do not need to speak. It is sufficient to say that Holy Houses of Masonry were everywhere in the land of France, and everywhere also were its royal standards unrolled. There is no question, from one point of view, that all the claims belonged to a world of dreams, that from old-world history they drew only its fables, from antique science its myths, that the dignities conferred in proceedings were delivered in a glass of faerie, and that the emblazoned programmer of high intent and purpose were apt to fade strangely and seem written in invisible ink under the cold light of fact. But the reality behind the dreams must be sought in the spirit of the dreamers, for whom something had happened which opened all the doors and unfolded amazing vistas of possibility on every side of them.

The man who held the keys and indeed had forged them was no other than Voltaire, who in this connection stands of course for an intellectual movement at large, which movement meant emancipation from the fetters of thought and action. To summarize the situation in a sentence, apart from the Church and its dogma, all things looked possible for a moment. The peculiar Masonic "system of morality, veiled in allegory and illustrated by symbols," might lead humanity either back to the perfection which it had lost or forward to that which it desired and could in mind describe dimly, however far away. The new prophets and their vaunted revelations might have God behind their gospels, and the darkness of the occult sciences might veil unknown Masters, rather than emissaries of perdition. Condemned practices, forbidden arts might lead through clouds of mystery into light of knowledge, and in this light history might call to be written out anew. We know at this day that Masonic legends are matters of fond invention, but some of them are old at the root, and we can understand in the eighteenth century how they came to pass as fact, more especially since the root of some was a Secret Tradition in Israel. When it came about, under circumstances which cannot be related here, that Masonic attention was drawn to the old Order of Knights Templar, which had been brought to the rack and the faggot as possessors of a strange knowledge drawn from the East, a Rite or a budget of Rites which claimed that the Order had never passed out of being was like a fortune to those who devised it.

It is from this point of view that we must survey the amazing growth of Masonry in all its multitude of forms. We shall conclude that it was pursued zealously, with a heart turned towards the truth, and as one who believes that he may not stand alone, I am not unprepared to think that some of the traditional histories, to us as monstrous growths, represented to the makers their views on the probability of things presented in the guise of myth. It was saved in this manner for them from the common charge of fraud. This is my judgment of the time, and there is one thing more on the wonder side of the subject, the expectations and the vistas seen in front. As the time drew on for Voltaire to be called away and when the chief High Grades of Masonry connoted a reaction from much that is typified by his name, there rose up another personality holding one key only, but it looked like *clavis abeconditorum a constitutione mundi*. This was Anton Mesmer, prominent in Parisian circles, a Mason like the rest of them, and destined presently to have more than one Grade enshrining his discovery and designed for the spread of its tenets. Granting the fact of his unseen but vital fluid, there was a root of truth at least in the long past of Magia, in the entrancements of vestal and pythoness, above all in occult medicine. So opened some other doors, and when Puysegur discovered clairvoyance again as it might be for a moment — the mystery of all the hiddenness looked on the point of unveiling. But the doors shut suddenly, the dreams and the epoch closed in the carnage of the French Revolution, and thereafter rose the baleful cresset of Corsica.

I have dwelt upon French Freemasonry because it is impossible to pass over it in presenting a picture of the period, but more especially because the life of the mystic Saint-Martin is bound up therewith for a certain number of years. Among the Rites which mattered at the moment his name connects with two, being the glory of the Strict Observance and the problematical Order of Elect Priesthood. Behead the first and there lies the mystery of its Unknown Superiors. But this, when reduced to its equivalent in simple fact, means the circumstances under which and the people by whom its root-matter was communicated in France to Baron von Hund, who returned with it to his German Fatherland and there formed it into a Rite, whose advent marked an epoch for evermore ill Masonry. But in respect of the second there lies behind it the claim of Pasqually's apostolate in that for which it stood and whence, if from anywhere, he derived on his own part — as, for example, the Rosy Cross. I cannot trace here the history of the

Strict Observance: it claimed to represent a perpetuation in secret of the Knights Templar and to be ruled by a hidden headship appertaining to that source. It may almost be said that it took Masonic Germany by storm, and planted its banners triumphantly all over Europe, save only in those British Isles where the Art and Craft of Emblematic Freemasonry rose up in 1717 among the taverns of London. It fell to pieces ultimately because it was in no better position to prove its claims than was the Craft itself to justify its recurrent appeals to the ancient past. But the point which concerns us is that before its karma overtook it the Rite was domiciled in France and had headquarters at Lyons under the government of a Provincial Grand Prior of Auvergne. It was transformed under these auspices from a Holy House of the Temple into a Spiritual House of God, in the keeping of a sacred chivalry pledged to the work of His glory and the promotion of peace on earth among all men of goodwill. It is the Apex of Masonry or the diadem of this Daughter of the Mysteries.

As regards Martines de Pasqually and his Rite des Elus Coens, or Order of the Elect Priesthood, he would seem to have been of Spanish descent or extraction, though he was born in Grenoble, and he is said to have been a coach-builder by trade — a piece of information which comes, however, from a hostile source. It may stand at its value and in any case does not signify, for it must be admitted, I believe, that he was of comparatively humble origin, and has extant letters swarm with orthographical errors, all has intellectual gifts notwithstanding, and also, has spiritual dedications. Whatever has been said to the contrary, it is quite certain — so far as there is evidence before us that he emerged into the light of his Masonic career for the first time in 1760 and that the place was Toulouse, where he presented himself at a certain Lodge, bearing a hieroglyphic charter and laying claim to occult powers. A year later he emerged again at Bordeaux where he appears to have been recognized on his own terms by another lodge, which he had satisfied in respect of his claims. In 1766 he proceeded to Paris and there laid the foundations of a Sovereign Tribunal, which included several prominent Masons. He was again at Bordeaux: in 1767, and three years later there are said to have been Lodges of his Rite not only in that city but at Montpellier, Avignon, La Rochelle, and Metz, as well as at Paris and Versailles. The Temple at Lyons was founded a little later.

Such is the external story of the Rite in bare outline, up to the time when for my present purpose — it can be merged in that of Saint-Martin. And now as to that for which it stood. I have intimated that Martines de Pasqually pretended to occult powers, and that there was at least one lodge which held that he had proved his claim. I shall show later the extent of our present knowledge respecting the content of his Rite. It had a certain ceremonial procedure, which — like all ritual — must have been sacramental in character, or with a certain meaning implied by its modes and forms; but only to the least extent was it otherwise veiled in allegory and illustrated by symbols. On the contrary, it was concerned with the communication of a secret doctrine by way of direct instruction and with a practice which must be called secret in the ordinary sense which attaches to the idea of occult art or science. The kind of practice was that which endeavors to establish communication with unseen intelligence by the observances of Ceremonial Magic. There was procedure of this kind during the Grades, or of some at least among them, and Pasqually, the Grand Sovereign, was also Grand Magus or Operator. It will be seen in a word that the Rite of Elect Priesthood had a very different undertaking in hand from anything embraced by the horizon of Craft Masonry or the rank and file of High Grades. The doctrine embodied a particular view concerning the Fall of Man and of all animated things belonging to the material order, it looked for the restoration of all, and on man as the divinely appointed agent of that great work to come.

EARLY LIFE OF THE MYSTIC

Louis Claude de Saint Martin belonged to the French nobility, as indicated by has armorial bearings and the coronet superposed thereon, but I have not come across his genealogy in any extant memorial. He was described very often in the past, and even by early French biographers, as the Marquis de Saint-Martin, but this is a mistake and has been rectified some time since: it does not appear that there was any title in has branch of the family. Though he suffered little inconvenience when the French Revolution came, he was included among the proscribed, meaning the noble classes. He was of Touraine stock and was born at Amboise in that district on January 18, 1743. It is said that his mother died soon after and that the father married again. We have his own evidence that familial respect was a sacred sentiment of his infancy; that all his happiness was perhaps due to has stepmother; that her teaching inspired him with love for God and man; and that the intercourse of their minds took place in perfect freedom.

There are various indications of his delicacy in early years, as when he tells us that he changed skins seven times in babyhood; that has body was a rough sketch; that he had very little "astral," meaning psychic force; that he could play passably on the violin, but that owing to physical weakness his fingers could not vibrate with sufficient power to make a cadence. I mention these points to show that, albeit Saint-Martin attained a fair age, he seems to have always been physically frail, amidst great mental activities. For the rest, there is no need to dwell upon his youth, as regards external facts, nor have many transpired. He was educated at the college of Pont-Leroy, was designed for the career of the law, and entered thereupon, but it proved so entirely distasteful that his father allowed him to exchange it for the profession of arms, he was then about twenty-two years of age.

On the inward side, or as regards his early dedications, we have the benefit of his own intimations, too brief and few as they are. There is a work of the past, by a writer named Abadie, on The Art of Self-Knowledge, and though on my own part I have not brought away from it any striking recollections, it had a certain reputation in its day. Saint-Martin tells us that he read it with delight in his youth, though he recognized later that it was characterized by sentiment rather than depth of thought. It was instrumental probably ill disposing him towards the life of contemplation and the following of the mystic path. There was also Burlamaqui, to whom he says that he owed his love for the natural basis of reason and human justice.

So far as regards books, but beyond these there were the promptings of his own spirit, and in respect of these he tells us that at the age of eighteen, amidst all the confusions of philosophy, he had attained certitude as to God and his own soul; that the seeker for wisdom had need of nothing more; that the foundation of all his happiness must be in contentment only with the truth; that absorption in material things was incomeprehensible for those who knew the treasures of reason and the spirit; that human science explained matter by matter, and that after its putative proofs there were other demonstrations needed; that the inmost prayer of his soul was for God to abide therein to the exclusion of all else, in which manner he came to see, thus early, that Divine Union is the true end of man; for I find this further thought set down as belonging to has first spiritual years, namely, that we are all widowed and that we are called to a second marriage.

The French Mystic and the Story of Modern Martinism

The influence of the Duc de Choiseul secured a commission for Saint-Martin in the regiment of Foix. The next three years of his life, which are practically a blank, so far as memorials are concerned, were filled with biographers, following obvious lines and those of least resistance. His occupations, in a word, were the duties of his profession and the study of religious philosophy. There is of course no question, and so far from the life of a soldier offering any barrier to his dedications, they opened a path before him which he followed with advantage for a certain distance and remembered his experience therein with unfailing affection and reverence. As we learn by his correspondence, Martines de Pasqually had married the niece of a retired major in the regiment of Foix, and he was known personally by the brother − officers of Saint- Martin, De Grainville among others, and in the end by Saint-Martin himself. De Grainville, De Balzac and Du Guers were initiates of the Elect Priesthood, and at some uncertain date between August 13 and October 2, 1768, Saint-Martin was received into the Order. According to his own testimony he had taken the first three Grades *en bloc*, apparently by verbal communication. They were conferred on him by M. de Balzac. There is no record as to how they impressed him, but among several references to the Grand Sovereign of the Rite on the part of his disciple for a period there is one which appertains more especially to the initial stage of their connection. "It is to Martines de Pasqually," says Saint-Martin, "that I owe my introduction to the higher truths." This sentence was written either on the eve of the Revolution or soon after and having regard to the spiritual distance travelled already by the witness, it is pregnant testimony.

As regards the Ritual-content of the Elect Priesthood, we know certainly about seven Grades, being Apprentice Elect Priest; Companion Elect Priest; Particular Master Elect Priest; Master Elect Priest; Grand Master Priests, otherwise Grand

Architects; Grand Elects of Zerubbabel; and a Grade of Rose Croix, not otherwise and more fully particularized, though it is a subject of frequent allusion in the correspondence of Martines de Pasqually and Saint Martin. In the year 1895, Papus, otherwise Dr. Gerard Encausse, testified that the "Rituals of the Elect Priests," with other numerous and important archives, had been transmitted as follows: To J.B. Willermoz, a merchant of Lyons, circa 1782. He was one of the successors of Pasqually and Grand Prior of Auvergne in the Strict Observance. From Willermoz to his nephew. From this nephew to his widow. From her to M. Cavernier, an unattached student of occultism. There are other documents held by the descendants of M. Jacques Matter, one of the earliest and most competent biographers of Saint-Martin. By the mediation of M. Elie Steel, a bookseller of Lyons, Papers was placed in communication with Cavernier, and was enabled to copy "the principal documents." Whether these included the Rituals does not appear, nor is it possible to indicate the present locality of the originals. It is certain, however, that Papus transcribed the Catechisms attached to six out of the seven Grades, as he published them at the date mentioned, and I have full evidence also that he conferred the Grade of Rose Crois on at least one occasion, some years subsequently, as we shall see more particularly at the close of the present monograph.

In the absence of the Rituals, which have never been printed, while I have failed to find manuscript copies in England, either in private hands or in any Masonic or other library, our available knowledge of the Grades is confined to the Catechisms and to the correspondence mentioned above. I will take these sources separately, as the first is concerned with the doctrine and symbolism of the Rite, and the second with its peculiar practices.

Apprentice Elect Priest — The instruction of this Grade imparted perfect knowledge — *en hypothesis* — on the existence of the Grand Architect of the Universe, on the principle of man's spiritual emanation and on having direct correspondence with his Master. It is obvious that the knowledge in question was conveyed dogmatically. As regards the origin of the Order, it derived from the Creator himself and had been perpetuated from the days of Adam, that is to say, from Adam to Noah, from Noah to Melchisedek, and afterwards to Abraham, Moses, Solomon, Zerubbabel and Christ. The meaning is that there has always been a Secret Tradition in the world, and its successive epochs are marked by successive custodians. It is in this sense also that the purpose of the Order is said to be the maintenance of man in his primeval virtue, his spiritual and divine powers.

Companion Elect Priest — Having been told of our "first estate" in the previous Degree, the Candidate hears in the next concerning the Fall of Man and personifies it in his own case. He has passed from the perpendicular to the triangle, or from union with his First Principle to the triplicity of material things. The Grade of Companion typifies this transition. The Candidate is engaged to counteract the work of the Fall, in which his own spirit has been undone, and his whole world is in travail thereupon, to "acquire the age of perfection." The root of all is in a living realization of what is implied by the first estate of man, his ambition, his lapse, and his punishment. There is one allusion to the pouring out of a more than human blood, but this subject is reserved to some later stage of advancement in the Order.

Particular Master Elect Priest — In the conventional symbolism, the Candidate passes from the triangle to the circles: he is at work in the circles of expiation, which are said to be six and in correspondence with six conceptions employed by the Great Architect in constructing the Universal Temple. The symbolism of the Temple of Solomon is explained in this

Degree, and its members are called to the practice of charity, good example, and all duties of the Order, for the reintegration of their individual principles, their Mercury, Sulphur, and Salt, in that unity of Divine Principles from which they first came forth. Here is the only distinct Hermetic reference found in the memorials of the Rite.

Elect Master — The Candidate enters the circle of reconciliation, and in common with his peers is engaged henceforward in warfare with the enemies of Divine Law and of man at large on earth. We hear also, but vaguely, concerning One Who is the Elect of God, Who has reconciled earth with man and all with the Grand Architect of the Universe. It is to be noted that in references of this kind we are left to infer that the Reconciler is Christ, for He is not mentioned by name. The Resurrection of Easter morning is referred to in similarly imprecise terms, and so also the sacrifice on Calvary. It transpires, however, that the warfare of the Grade is against the enemies of the Christian Religion. The initiations and adornments of Craft Masonry have been stigmatized as apocryphal in the first Grade, and yet they were sufficiently essential to be conferred invariably in summary form on every Candidate for the Elect Priesthood — presumably in cases where they had not been taken previously. In the Grade of Elect Master he is warned to cut himself off from all clandestine secret societies, communicating apocryphal instructions, which are "contrary to Divine Law and to the Order."

Grand Master Priests, surnamed Grand Architects. — The Candidate was thirty-three years old in the fourth Grade and he has now attained the age of eighty. It would seem that he receives some kind of ordination. It is a Grade of light, and the Temple is ablaze with light. There are four Wardens, who represent the four symbolical Angels of the four quarters of heaven, recalling the occult mystery of the Enochian Tablets, according to the memorials of Dr. John Dee in The Faithful Relation. The ordination — whatever its form — is said to be operated by the thought and will of the Eternal, and by the power, word, and intention of His deputies. The members of this Grade are occupied with the purification of their physical senses so that they may participate in the work of the spirit. They are engaged otherwise in constructing new Tabernacles and rebuilding old. There are said to be four kinds of Tabernacles in the Universal Temple, being the body of man, the body of woman, the Tabernacle of Moses, and that of the Sun, or the "temporal spiritual" Tabernacle which the Great Architect of the Universe "has destined to contain the sacred names and words of material and spiritual reaction, distinguished by wisdom as by a torch of universal temporal life." There is no further allusion to this Spiritual Sun. The Candidate now hears the Name of Christ, apparently for the first time in his progress through the Rite. It must be said that the Catechisms are rather obscure documents, and inferences drawn there from as to procedure in the Rituals are therefore precarious, but it would seem that the Candidate in this Degree begins to take part in those magical operations which are the chief concern of the Rite, as we shall see.

Grand Elect of Zerubbabel — The Prince of the People is represented as a type of Christ and his work as typical of redemption. In the Masonic Grade known as the Royal Arch the Candidate testifies that he belongs to the tribe of Judah, but a Grand Elect on the contrary protests such an imputation. He is of the tribe of Ephraim, described as that which has always enjoyed freedom, and the last of the tribes of Israel but the first of the Elect. His earthly age is defined to be seventy years, while that of his spiritual election is seven. The seventy years of captivity are those of material life, or life apart from election and from the ordination of true priesthood. The election attained by the Candidate imposes on him the spiritualization of his material passions, the conquest of the enemies of truth and those also of liberty. His rank is friend of God, protector of virtue and professor of truth. It is to be noted that he has had no part in the building of the Second Temple, because it was a type only of that Temple of our humanity which none, but the Spirit can rebuild. This being so, it is difficult to see why members of the Grade are called Grand Elects of Zerubbabel.

Grade of Rose Croix — particulars of which are wanting, as already seen, there being no Catechism extant. But the true Rose Croix is of Christ, and without it Pasqually's Rite would have been left at a loose end, for it looked through all its Grades to that Divine Event which ushered in the Christian Era.

In the above enumeration respecting the content of the Rite I have taken its Catechisms as my guide, but it remains to add that there is some confusion on the subject. A letter of the Grand Sovereign has been quoted under date of June 16, 1760, in which the Grades are set out according to the following list: Apprentice, Companion, Particular Master, Grand Elect Master, Apprentice Priest, Companion Priest, Master Priest, Grand Master Architect. To these Ragon added a Grade of Knight Commander, which Papus seeks to identify with that of Rose Croix. I find no trace of the letter in published Pasqually memorials, and the date is certainly wrong. As regards Ragon, his mammoth lists of Degrees, Rites and Orders are utterly uncritical, but the fact that in this case he produces an enumeration which is corroborated somewhere in the unpublished correspondence of the Grand Sovereign may justify us in thinking that there is authority for the ninth item and that the entire scheme may have represented an early state of Pasqually's Masonic plan. There is in any case the fullest evidence that his Rite was at work when several of its Ceremonies were only in an embryonic stage. I also observe that in a letter of Saint Martin dated May 20, 1771, there is reference to a degree under the initials G.R., which corresponds to no title extant in either scheme, as it is certainly not Rose Croix, this being always represented by R in Saint-Martin's correspondence. Amidst variations and uncertainties, we are, I think, justified in regarding the Grade Names at the head of the several Catechisms as those appertaining to the Rite in its completed form.

On the surface of these documents there is nothing to suggest that the Grades to which they are attributed related to Ceremonial Magic. They belong to the part of doctrine and the part also of symbolism, the latter including official secrets signs, tokens, words, and similar accidents of purely Masonic convention. For the practical part we must have recourse to the correspondence of Pasqually and — as it may seem — perhaps curiously, to that of Saint-Martin. The letters of both were addressed to Jean-Baptiste Willermoz, the merchant of Lyons, who appears to have held the rank of Inspector-General in 1767, though more than a year later he is denominated Apprentice Rose Croix. It would seem therefore that the jurisdiction implied by the broader title could have been exercised only over lower Grades of the Order. On August 13, 1768, the Grand Sovereign began to instruct Willermoz in occult or magical procedure and continued to do so at long intervals until 1772, the communications in all being ten in number, so far as they have become available in published works. The operations imposed were to be performed by Willermoz in the solitude of a private room and have therefore nothing to do with ceremonial observance in Lodge or Temple. The practice in these — for it appears that there was a practice — seems to have been performed by Pasqually himself, looking forward presumably to that time when some of his disciples would have developed occult powers under his tuition and would be qualified to operate on their own part in public, so to speak, with some assurance of success.

The Ceremonial Magic was Christian and presupposed throughout the efficacy of religious formulae consecrated from time immemorial by the usage of the Latin Church. The instructions reduced into summary form may be presented thus: The Novice was covenanted to abstain from flesh meat, apparently of all kinds, for the rest of his life. As an Apprentice Rose Croix he was forbidden occult work except for three days in succession at the beginning of either equinox, meaning three days before the full moon of March and September. As regards spiritual preparation, he must recite the Office of the Holy Spirit every Thursday at any hour of the day; the *Miserere mei*, standing in the center of the room at night before retiring, facing East; and the De Profundis on both knees and with face bowed to the ground. The clothing prescribed is elaborate, including all insignia of the Order that the Novice was entitled to wear, but here it will be sufficient to say that as he must be deprived of all metals, even pins, he removed his ordinary clothing except vest, drawers, socks and felt slippers. Over these he placed a white *alb*, with broad flame-colored borders. He described the segment of a circle on the East side of the room and a complete circle of retreat on the West side, placing the proper inscriptions at the proper points, with the symbols and wax tapers. These arrangements completed, he prostrated himself at full length within the western circle in complete darkness, for a space of six minutes, after which he arose and lighted all the tapers belonging to that circle. He then prostrated himself within the eastern segment, pronouncing one of the Names inscribed thereon and supplicating God, in virtue of the power given to His servants here reciting all the inscribed angelic names — to grant that which was desired by the Novice with humble and contrite heart. The Novice again rose up and performed other operations, including a particular kind of incense and the recital of certain invocations which are not given in the text. The operation was to last one hour and a half, onward from midnight, no food having been taken since noon. There are other directions, not always in harmony with those which preceded, but the instruction is left unfinished, and as regards these initial operations we do not know what purpose they served or what manifestations characterized success therein.

About two years later Pasqually supplied further directions of a more advanced or at least more elaborate kind, the circle of retreat being now located in the center of the room; but again, the procedure depends on particulars which have been sent previously and the nature of which is unknown. We hear also of visions, described as white, blue, clear ruddy white, and so forth; of visible sparks, of goose-flesh sensations, as of things seen and felt by mere novices of the Order. As to purpose, however, and result there is still nothing that transpires, except indeed the complete failure of Willermoz to obtain any satisfaction. The letters of Saint-Martin to the same correspondent on the same subject may be said practically to begin as those of Pasqually ended, and they are models of clear exposition, compared with those of the Grand Sovereign. They endeavor in the first place to encourage Willermoz and dissuade him from supposing either that he is himself to blame or that the occult ceremonies are invalid. At an early stage one of them was accompanied by "the grand ceremonial" of the Grand Architects, a complete plan of this Grade and a prayer or invocation for daily use. We hear also of a "simple form of ordination" under the initials G.R., to which I have alluded previously; of extended and reduced versions of some Grades; of Elect and Priestly Grades. There are references to Latin originals of certain workings; to procedure with Candidates, on their reception as Grand Architects, evidently magical in character; forms of conjuration and exorcism of evil spirits which do not differ generically from those of historical Rituals; and much on the formation of circles, with their proper modes of inscription. These things do not extend our knowledge, except upon points of detail, and after midsummer, 1773, the character of the correspondence changes. Saint-Martin had supplied for a period the place, as it were, of a secretary to his occult Master, but Pasqually was called to St. Domingo in 1772 on "temporal business" of his own and was destined never to return.

It follows that the Ceremonial Magic of the Elect Priesthood is by no means fully available from published sources; but so far as the procedure is before us it does not differ, as I have intimated, from the common records of the art except as these records differ one from another. This being the case, and as most of us are acquainted with the preposterous concerns of Art Magic in the past, we have, in the next place, to account as we can for an opinion on has early school expressed by Saint-Martin long after he had abandoned it and all its ways: "I will not conceal from you that in the school through which I passed, now more than twenty-five years ago, communications of all kinds were numerous and frequent, that I had my share in these like all the others, and that every sign indicative of the Repairer was found therein." He said also: "There were precious things in our first school, and I am even disposed to believe that M. Pasqually, to whom you allude and who, since it must be said, was our Master, had the active key of all that our dear Bohme sets forth in his theories, but that he did not regard us as fitted for such high truths." In the peculiar terminology of Saint- Martin, the Repairer signified Christ, and what therefore were those "communications" obtained as the result of invocations recited in magical circles drawn with chalk on the floor and inscribed, as in the devices of old sorcery, with more or less unintelligible names? After what manner precisely did they manifest or at least indicate the presence of Christ? For an answer to these questions, we depend on the accuracy of a single witness who was either in possession of many priceless unpublished documents or had access thereto as President of the Martinist Order — the late Gerard Encausse, otherwise Dr. Papus — to whom my notes have referred already. He presents us with further extracts from the letters of Martines de

Pasqually, who affirms therein that if the thing — *La chose* — were not as I have certified and had it not been manifested as it was, not only in my own presence but in that of so many others who desired to know it, I should have abandoned it myself and should have been in conscience bound to dissuade those who approached it in good faith; that ill respect of the failure of Willermoz there was no ground for surprise because "the Thing is sometimes severe towards those who desire it too ardently before the time." One would think that *La chose* simply signified the subject or matter in hand, but according to Papus it was the Intelligence or Mysterious Being which manifested in response to the invocations. We are to interpret the reference in this sense when Saint-Martin says, in his communication to Willermoz of March 25, 1771, that he was "convinced concerning the thing before having received the most efficacious of our ordinations." I do not know how Papus satisfied himself respecting this forced and arbitrary construction, but whether it is correct or not, there is no question as to the fact that a Mysterious Being manifested by the evidence of the archives or that it was called subsequently by other names, such as "the Unknown Agent charged with the work of initiation," an expression of Willermoz.

It follows that we have good ground for accepting the view of Abbe Fournie, another disciple of the Rite, when he said that Pasqually had the faculty of confirming his instructions by means of "external visions, at first vague and passing with the rapidity of lightning, but afterwards more and more distinct and prolonged." Having established this point of fact, which sufficiently distinguishes the Grand Sovereign from other purveyors of High Masonic Grades in France of the eighteenth century, and his Rite also from many scores of contemporary institutions, we have to ascertain — if we can — what characterized the manifestations, so that they justified Saint-Martin in the extraordinary view which he held concerning them, not in the first flush of occult experiences, but at a mature period of life.

Meanwhile I have sketched his position and environment at the beginning of his intellectual career. As a result of exchanging the profession of law for that of arms, he had entered a circle which brought him to the gates of certain Instituted Mysteries, then at work about him; he had been initiated, passed, and raised in the parlance of Blue Masonry; he had received the ordination of the Elect Priesthood; and had attained its highest Grade, being that of Rose Croix. It remains to add that he had left the army and was now approaching a point where the road which he had travelled divided: he had therefore to choose a path.

THE SEARCH AFTER TRUTH

The correspondence between Saint-Martin and Willermoz continued for two years and five months, but they had never seen one another. In the early part of September 1773, Saint-Martin repaired to Lyons and was domiciled in that town for something approaching a year, during part of which he was apparently the guest of his rich Masonic brother. His own resources were small, and there are indications that he was not on the best terms with his father, no doubt because for the second time he had abandoned a career in life. We have seen that there was a Temple of the Elect Priesthood at Lyons, which was also an historically important center of Freemasonry in France, and Willermoz was an active member and officer of all the Rites. Saint-Martin, on the other hand, cared little or less than nothing for ceremonial procedure, for Ritual which he found empty and for the hollow pomp of titles. According to his own evidence, the offices of Ceremonial Magic were only less distasteful, notwithstanding his high opinion of the influences at work among them in the circle to which he belonged. He affirms that he had no "vitality" in activities of that kind; that he had little "talent" for its operations; that he "experienced at all times so strong an inclination to the intimate secret way that this external one never seduced me further, even in my youth"; and that he exclaimed more than once to has Master: "Can all this be needed to find God?" Such being the case, there need be no cause for surprise that Saint-Martin put on record long after has opinion that the "first sojourn at Lyons in 1773" was not much more "profitable" than others which he made later and especially in 1785. It was important, however, in another and very different way, for it marked the beginning of his literary life. "It was at Lyons," he tells us, "that I wrote the book *Des Erreurs et de la Verite*, partly by way of occupation and because I was indignant with the philosophers so called, having read in Boulanger that the origin of religions was to be sought in the terror occasioned by the catastrophes of Nature. I wrote some thirty pages at first, which I showed to a circle that I was instructing at the house of M. Willermoz, and they pledged me to continue. It was composed towards the end of 1773 and at the beginning of 1774, in the space of four months and by the kitchen-fire, for there was no other at which I could warm myself.

He was not therefore in residence during those months with his Masonic friend: he was probably in a pension somewhere, and not too well situated because of his means. The task was executed with great expedition, having regard to its subject and the deep searching demanded throughout its length: indeed, his application must have been unremitting, the result comprising nearly five hundred pages. The next point which it is requisite to note, for reasons which will appear immediately, is that it is written in the first person, which indeed recurs continually, so that the Philosophe Inconnu whose name appears on the title is with the reader from beginning to end. The individual note was characteristic of

Saint-Martin's writings throughout his literary life, but it is to be observed that though ever present it was never insistent and was never touched by egotism. He spoke from the fullness of the heart, as from an unfailing fountain, and has even put on record his feeling that there was not enough paper in the world to contain all that he had to deliver, could he only reduce it to writing. He also had a certain sacred tenderness towards the children of his mind, even when he dwelt on their imperfections. In a word, he was a typical literary man of the better kind, as well as a true mystic.

We are told elsewhere that his works, and especially the earliest in time, were the fruit of his affectionate attachment to man, and that as regards *Des Errears et de la Verite*, being concerned only with making war on materialistic philosophy, he could not permit the reader to see precisely where he was being led, because it would have set him at once in opposition, "the Scriptures having fallen into such discredit among men." It follows not only that they are not quoted in the work; but that Christ Himself is referred to in a veiled manner, as the Active and Intelligent Cause, the Agent, Guide of Man, etc. It would be easy to enumerate other points, showing that Saint-Martin's first work was schemed and excogitated and written from his own basis, under one reserve only, that the root-matter of its doctrine is presented as coming from a secret source, that he was under pledges concerning it and that owing to these a reservation was imposed upon him, so that his elucidations could be carried only to a certain point. Here is a clear issue, and as regards the source itself we are not in doubt concerning it, since the year 1899, when Martinez de Pasqually's important *Traite de la Reintegration des Etres* was published for the first time in France. It is practically possible to check every point of reticence registered by Saint-Martin and to see what lies behind it by reference to this treatise, it being understood that Pasqually on his own part derived from other teachers to us unknowns with whom he seems to have been in personal communication, but whether in the body or out of the body we cannot tell.

Having presented the literary history of *Des Erreurs* in this manner, I have now to contrast with it the counter-view put forward by Dr. Papus on the alleged authority of his Martinist archives. He affirms, that the book *Des Erreurs* was due almost entirely to an "invisible origin"; that the being whom in 1895 he had certified as "always designated under the enigmatic name of La chose" was called the Unknown Philosopher; that it was he who gave forth the work as regards the major part; that he dictated 166 cahiers d'instruction; that some of these were transcribed by Saint-Martin; that the "Unknown Philosopher" gave orders for Saint-Martin to assume this name; and that the said "Agent" himself destroyed about eighty cahiers in 1790 to prevent them falling into the hands of Robespierre's emissaries, "who were making unheard-of efforts to acquire them." It follows that Saint- Martin has given an altogether misleading account of his first book, and that despite its strong and prevailing personal note it cannot be called his work. I have, however, collated his statements, and those who know him are likely to prefer his version of the matter to archives largely unpublished and not available for inspection, as Dr. Papus refers expressly to documents reserved for the sole use of the directing Committee at the head of his Supreme Council. When, therefore, he states further that the archives include various sheets of instructions communicated by "the Unknown Agent" and annotated by the hand of Saint Martin we must regard it in the light of later revelations supplied by the President of the Martinist Order, remembering that in 1899 he promised to produce proofs in a volume devoted to the mystic. That volume appeared in 1902 and contained fifty unpublished letters of Saint-Martin, to some of which I have referred. They are prefaced by a biographical summary written around the documents. In neither one nor the other is any ray of light cast upon the previous claims: they are indeed the subject of allusion only in a single sentence. But we obtain unexpected enlightenment in other respects. Whereas there is no evidence whatever of communications dictated by the Unknown Agent during the life of Pasqually or for over ten years after his death, we are told by Dr. Papus, though there is no allusion to the fact in Saint-Martz's letters, that in 1785, the Agent in question, who seems to have remained in abeyance since the death of the Grand Sovereign, began to manifest at Lyons, where he dictated "nearly one hundred folios," being those precisely of which the majority were burned in 1790. The archives of the Order, it is added, include the bulk of those that were saved. In place, moreover, of leaving seen, transcribed and annotated a mass of written instructions prior to 1785, we are told only of teachings that are likely to have been "heard" and to have been incorporated into his work by the author of *Des Erreurs*.

It will be seen that the ground vs. changed completely and that we are getting nearer to the probable facts of the case. I do not doubt that Willermoz and his circle received psychic communications in one or another psychic condition, induced by prolonged operations inspired by that intent, or with the aid of "lucids," the intervention of whom is admitted. I do not doubt that they were reduced into writing, and as the news of what was takings place brought Saint-Martin to Lyons with all possible speed, it is certain that he read, he may well have transcribed and annotated, but all this was years subsequently to the publication of *Des Erreurs et de la Verite*. I am preferring no charge whatever against Dr. Papus, who sealed a laborious life by a heroic death in the cause of the sick and wounded during the Great War. We were, moreover, personally acquainted, and our relations were always cordial. But he was unfortunately a most inaccurate writer, and the present monograph might be extended to twice its size if I analyzed the errors which fill his three books dealing with Martinist subjects. As regards the archives, he tells us in 1895 that he had been permitted to see those which were in the possession of a certain M. Cavernier and had transcribed some of them, devoting one week to the task. In 1899 it looks as if some originals had come into his possession, though he does not explain how. I conceive that in this year he was in confusion as to the dates, extent, and precise nature of the psychic communications. By 1902 he had made better progress with them and modified his affirmations accordingly, but without overtly withdrawing anything. I conceive that in this manner the question may be permitted to rest, unless and until the present custodians of the archives decide to proceed further with the work of their publication. It seems to me that I have adopted a reasonable and middle ground which accounts for the facts without accusing anyone. Under the aegis of Pasqually the Rite of the Elect Priesthood was one of occult instruction as well as occult practice and the pageant - such as it may have been — of cumulative Grades. The teaching was of course under pledges, and that part of it which Saint-Martin felt permitted to unfold was put forward in his first book. La chose may refer to Pasqually's Guide in the unseen, howsoever communication was established — supposing that Papus is correct in his understanding of this term. But the pledges may have also covered instruction from other sources, the "Predecessors" about whom Pasqually we owe to Willermoz on April 13, 1768. I take it that the sum of instruction received from all sources is enshrined in the Grand Sovereign's Treatise on Reintegration.

We have seen that it is reflected also in the first work of Saint-Martin, as through the alembic of an original mind, disposed already to the higher elections of the human soul. A work of collation would bear this fact in mind, but there is no opportunity to attempt it in the present place. Saint-Martin's theory of good and evil is based on the doctrine of two unequal principles, between which there is no co-operation and no analogy. Of these two the inferior became evil by the sole act of its own will, being one of opposition to the Eternal Will of Goodness, wherein is essential unity. Man in his primal estate is the most ancient of all beings in that which is understood as Nature, but he was the last which entered its scheme. He came forth from the center, that is to say, from the Divine Goodness, but abode in the presence thereof, and his function was intended to be that of leading all things back into unity. But he fell from this high estate, was deprived of all his ancient rights, while another agent was commissioned to take his place. This agent is the active and intelligent cause, and thereunto, as the Great Chief and Guide, is committed to the order of the universe. The inference is that this order was intended originally to have been in the hands of man until ad that is in separation shall have been reconciled with its one and only source. It is to be inferred that he or that which has been called to rule in substitution for man has become the leader into unity, otherwise the reconciler and repairer, while his most important charge since that which is termed the Fall is the reconciliation of our fallen race. We have passed from unity into separation by the work of our own will, have renounced our own vocation and forfeited all our titles; but he who repairs restores, in virtue of a capacity for restoration which has always remained with us. It follows that at the time of reintegration the estate of man will be in virtual unity with that of the Repairer, whose true name is Christ, whereas Saint-Martin says that in respect of our potencies we are all Christs. Saint-Martin's expositions are like Craft Freemasonry, "veiled in allegory and illustrated by symbols." The nature of the Fall is clouded in this manner, for it is said that man descended into the region of fathers and mothers, otherwise into the circle of physical generation, in place of those generations which are spiritual. It is a parable of original unity and subsequent divorce, of the separation between subject and object, or of the lover and beloved in another form of imagery. Now, the way of division is the way of errors, but that of truth is the way of union, or this at least is how I understand Saint-Martin in the testimonies which he bears to reality. In a sense his first work is de omnibus rebus, but here is the root of all. Having regard to its suggestive presentation, to its originality of thought and style, and — not least of all — to its studied reservations and allusions to a hidden source of knowledge, I can understand its extraordinary effect upon prepared minds of France in the year 1776.

A DOCTRINE OF CORRESPONDENCES

We have seen that Saint-Martin completed his literary experiment in the early part of 1774, and in the autumn of that year he paid a short visit to Italy, in the company of a brother of Willermoz. They returned apparently to Lyons, where Saint-Martin must have been occupied for some time in seeing his work through the press. It appeared in 1775 under the pseudonym of "the Unknown Philosopher," and bearing the imprint of Edinburgh, which, however, must be understood as Lyons. We do not know when he left that city, but he was in Paris at the end of July, at Lyons again in the autumns at Tours on a flying visit, and then at Bordeaux in 1776. He had returned to Paris in March 1777. Pasqually died at Port-au-Prince on September 20, 1774, having nominated Caignet de Lestere as his successor, he also being resident in the West Indies. The Temples of the Elect Priesthood were left to their own devices, and the mighty pageant of the Strict Observance drew several under that obedience. Willermoz becomes — as stated previously — Grand Prior of Auvergne and having profited nothing in attempting to follow Pasqually's instructions concerning Ceremonial Magic, he was presumably more and more immersed in Masonry, especially its High Grades. Whatever sympathy may have existed originally between him and Saint-Martin when they were merely correspondents —

their paths were now dividing, and the born mystic was disposing of the occult yoke placed upon him by his early Master. There is evidence of strained relations when Saint-Martin wrote from Paris on July 30, 1775, to dissuade Willermoz from supposing that he was seeking the latter's conversion to his own views or was presuming to pronounce judgment upon him. At the same time certain matters, the nature of which does not emerge in the letter, made it necessary for the peace of both that he should no longer be a guest of has friend, though for the sake of the Order and its — members he must return to Lyons and remain there a given time. It should not appear, in other words, that there was estrangement between himself and Willermoz. When, therefore, he took a lodging in isolation, it would be explained that he was following up chemical experiments. Whether the device served its purpose we do not know, but after it reached a term the two correspondents do not seem to have met one another for ten years. They continued to write occasionally, and they remained friends.

It has been suggested that *Des Erreurs* filled the purse of Saint-Martin, but the evidence of his improved position cannot be accounted for by reference to that source, its considerable measure of success notwithstanding. On the contrary, there are indications that he was on better terms with his father, and I infer that thenceforward he was not without modest means. It has been suggested also that the authorship of the book was kept a profound secret. This is unlikely in the nature of things, for it was obviously well known at Lyons prior to publication. It has been said by one of his biographers that he "became known widely and was in request everywhere." His own memorial notes bear witness to the distinguished circle of his acquaintances, and so also do his letters. It is unnecessary to labor the point, and as, for the rest, his life in social and intellectual circles during the seven years between 1775 and

1782 has left little trace behind it, I pass on to the latter date, to which his second book belongs. In one of those unconverted intimations which seem to open for a moment his whole heart of purpose, Saint-Martin says that his work has its fount and course in the Divine. He is alluding to work of life rather than books, but it is true of all that he wrote, and the Tableau Naturel des Rapports qui existent entre *Dieu, l'Homme et Univers* was assuredly undertaken for the justification by means of their unfolding of the ways of God to man. It was written in Paris, as he tells us, partly in Luxembourg at the house of the Marquise de Lusignan, and partly in that of the Marquise de la Croix. Publication took place in two parts appearing, as previously, in one volume elated 1782 — at the symbolical Edinburgh, which on this occasion is more likely to mean Paris than Lyons though the latter place is understood by bibliographers. We have seen that *Des Erreurs* confessed to recurring reservations, and it has all the atmosphere of a truncated document issued from a Temple of the Mysteries, or at least a Secret College. The Natural Scheme of Correspondences, on the surface, withholding nothing, yet it adopts another air of mystery. The entirely anonymous publishers state in a prefatory note that they received the MS. from an unknown person; that it had numerous marginal additions in a different hand; that they seemed different from the rest of the work; and that in printing they had been placed in quotation commas, to distinguish them from the rest of the text. When tested on the subject by Baron de Liebistorf, Saint-Martin admitted that the passages referred to were his; that the publisher regarded them as out of keeping with the rest of the work; that he gave the explanation which he did to prepare readers; and that he was allowed to have his way. It happens that the paragraphs in quotations are the most enigmatical parts of the work and suggest derivation from Pasqually's occult instructions; it happens also that Saint-Martin was replying to a correspondent who was not initiated; and if, therefore, what he says does not quite cover the facts, we may take it as the best that he could do without discovering his source. In any case, the paragraphs were written — i.e., expressed — by himself, and, for the rest, their consequence is not in proportion to their obscurity.

The Tableau compares the universe to a great temple: "the stars are its lights, the earth is its altar, all corporeal beings are its holocausts, and man, who is priest of the Eternal, offers the sacrifices." It follows from the logic of the symbolism that he himself is the chief holocaust, and this must be the sense in which it is said also that the universe is "like a great fire lighted since the beginning of things for the purification of all corrupted beings." Finally, it is "a great allegory or fable which must give place to a grand morality." When it is affirmed elsewhere that the external world is illusory, the reference presumably is to its surface sense, apart from the inward meaning. God is the meaning and God the grand morality; creation is not merely His visible sign, but a channel through which His thoughts are communicated to intelligent beings. Here is the only mode of communication for fallen man, namely, through signs and emblems. But these and the whole signifying universe are earnests of God's love for corrupted creatures and evidence that He is at work unceasingly "to remove the separation so contrary to their felicity." As it is certain that He does not world in vain, it follows that a day will come when there shall be no separateness thenceforward. So does the end emerge with all true thought implying — when it does not express — the doctrine of unity, all true paths being paths that lead thereto, and God Himself — One, Immutable and Eternal — the Witness from everlasting to this our end of being. Here is the Great Work, and it is to be performed "by restoring in our faculties the same law, the same order, the same regularity by which all beings are directed in Nature," or, in other words, by acting no longer in our own name, but in that of the living God. It is a work of the will in its redirection, for this is the agent bar which alone man and every free being can efface within them and round them the traces of error and crime. The revindication of the will is therefore the chief work of all fallen creatures.

The same lesson is conveyed in symbolical language when it is said that "the object of man on earth is to employ all rights and powers of his being in rarefying as far as possible the intervening media between himself and the true Sun, so that — the opposition being practically none there may be a free passage, and that the rays of light may reach him without refraction." It will be seen that, as in *Des Erreurs*, the instrument by which we fall is that by which we must rise: the evil in man originated in the will of man, and thereby it must be stamped out his "crime" is defined as "the abuse of the knowledge he possessed concerning the union of the principle of the universe with the universe." His penalty was the privation of this knowledge. The definition is dogmatic, and it is obvious that Saint-Martin can throw no light on the real nature of the alleged knowledge: otherwise, he must have undone the crime in his own person. He is least convincing when discussing the legendary Fall, and most when conveying his own thoughts apart from any formal system. When he tells us that truth is in God, that it is written in all about us, that its messages are meant for our reading, that the light within leads to the light without; that the principle of being and of life is within us, that it cannot perish, that the regeneration of our "virtues" is possible; and that we can ascend to a demonstration of the Active and Invisible Principle, from which the universe derives its existence and its laws: we are then in the presence of the mystic who is speaking on the warrants of his proper insight.

THE MAN OF DESIRE

After the publication of *Le Tableau Naturel* Saint-Martin remained more or less at Pares, and his intermittent correspondence with Willermoz is at times scarcely intelligible in the absence of the latter's communications. Willermoz evidently was passing through a strenuous period, connected perhaps with embroilments consequent on the Masonic Convention of Wilhelmsbad, held in 1782, and the fate of the Strict Observance. There is one allusion which suggests vaguely his transformation of that Rite at Lyons prior to 1778, and the creation thereby of the Knights Beneficent of the Holy City. But there is no certainty on the subject, and for the rest we learn only of Saint-Martin's brief interest in the discovery of Mesmer, its connection with a society instituted by that great comet of a season, and his presence at certain cures operated magnetically by Puysegur. A single remark informs us that he would take no part in the Convention of Paris, summoned by the Rite of the Philalethes. We reach in this manner the month of April, 1785, when Saint Martin had received such news from Willermoz that in his reply of the 29th he expresses his rapture on learning that the sun has risen on Israel; he affirms that the man so chosen is for him henceforward a man of God whom he will venerate as the anointed one of the Savior; he entreats him to pardon whatever wrongs he may be thought to have committed against him on his own part; he ascribes all differences which have arisen between them to his own ignorance he condemns himself for his temerity in having published anything; he asks Willermoz to intercede for him with something which appears to be called *La chose*, whose place he has taken unasked; he prays to be enlightened on the faults of his own heart the errors of his mind and of his works, he places himself under has orders and terms him has master, holy friend, father in God and Christ Jesus.

It looks evident in a word that Saint-Martin stood ready to set aside all his previous views and inferentially those which had always disposed him towards the inward way of the mystics rather than that of his first Master What, therefore, had occurred? I have forestalled the event unavoidably in my third chapter. According to Dr. Papus, the archives in his possession show that after prolonged failure Willermoz reached the end of his labors, that he obtained "phenomena of the highest importance," which culminated in 1785, or "thirteen years after the death of his initiator Martines de Pasqually." More explicitly, the Being who is said to be described by Willermoz as "the Unknown Agent charged with the work of initiation" - otherwise, perhaps, *La chose* — materialized at Lyons and gave instructions which — as we have seen were reduced to writing.

Occurrences of this kind being innumerable at the present day, I suppose that we are not able to sympathize with the raptures of Saint-Martin, his tears or his changing front. His next letter, dated May 13, indicates that he had been reassured and consoled by Willermoz, for which he praises God. He waits now on a summons to Lyons, that he may see and hear for himself. Meanwhile he and his correspondent will remain united through time and eternity. On June 30 he has made preparations for the journey and is looking to greet Willermoz soon after the letter on that date. Of what followed we know little and next to nothing, except that fifteen months later Saint-Martin is in Paris, bewailing his imprudence in having spoken too freely to certain brethren and thus prejudiced the "enjoyments" of has friend. In January 1787, he is in London, where he remained for some six months, making the acquaintance of William Law and the astronomer Herschel, the Comte de Divonne, Dutens and the Russian Prince Galitzin, with whom he was domiciled. It was in London also, as he tells us, that he wrote his third book, *L'Homme de Desir*, though it was not published till 1790, and then at Lyons. It is important not only in itself, as one of Saint-Martin's most inspired writings, but as showing beyond debate that, whatever experiences had awaited him at Lyons, they cooled the enthusiasm kindled by their first indications, and he had returned to his own path with an increased sense of dedication. I can say only that the hunger and thirst after God are in all its pages. This is not, however, to suggest that he is denuded of all interest in the Lyons phenomena: his only letter written to Willermoz while in England offers a contrary indication; but the interest appears detached.

In July 1787, Saint-Martin passed through Paris on his way to Amboise, where his father had been stricken with paralysis. In September he was again at Lyons, but it was in the absence of Willermoz. Thereafter he paid a second visit to Italy, visiting Siena and Rome. In the early part of 1788 Papus reports that the apparitions of the Agent had ceased, according to a letter of Willermoz. In April of that year Saint-Martin is in Paris and about to visit his father, who is still alive, at the native place of both. In June he proceeded to Strasbourg, where he resided for three years, the happiest of all his life. As I said long ago: "It was here, under the auspices of Rodolphe Salzmann, also mystically disposed, and of Madame de Boecklin, his most intimate and cherished woman friend, that he made his first acquaintance with the writings of Jacob Bohme; here he became intimate with the Chevalier de Silferhielm, a nephew of Swedenborg; and all his horizon widened under the influence of the Teutonic theosopher. On December 16, 1789, he asked Willermoz whether he could participate in the "initiation" attached to the Regime Rectifie without belonging to its Symbolical Lodge. I do not think that Papus knew what this meant, and therefore wisely offered no word of comment. But the *Regime Ecossais Ancien et Rectifie* was the Strict Observance as transformed at Lyons and ratified at Wilhelmsbad; more especially it was the Craft Degrees of this Rite and their supplement the Grade of St. Andrew. Beyond it were the novitiate and chivalry of the Holy City, and these again beyond were two final Grades, which I do not propose to specify by name, as they were and are in obscurity. It is to these that Saint-Martin refers under the vague title of "initiations." He did not apparently get a straight answer, and on July 4, 1790, he asked Willermoz to advise the proper quarter of his resignation from the Interior Order — i.e., the novitiate and chivalry — and from all lists and registers in which his name may have been inscribed since 1785. He points out that in the spirit he had never been integrated therein. His intention apparently was to remain among the Coens — i.e., the Elect Priesthood — but how nominally we call imagine from the utter detachment of his letter, the references to his simple mode of life, and above all his closing words, in which he registers a hope that he has separated for ever from those complicated paths which had always wearied him. It is an eloquent commentary on the manifestations of Lyons, the dictated instructions of *La chose*, the astral travelling of D'Hauterive, and the clairvoyance's of the "lucids" who seem to have assisted at the operations. There are no further letters from Saint-Martin to Willermoz, and already during this year, in some early month, the Agent had received "on demand" and had destroyed "more than eighty folios" of his dictated instructions, the same not having been "published," as Willermoz states in a letter quoted by Papus.

It follows that "the Unknown Agent charged with the work of initiation" had undone that work, and whether, as suggested — but Papus seems doubtful — the manifestations continued at intervals till 1796, it would seem that there is no record of proceedings, and the whole thing sagged out. The Elect Priesthood missed its mark; with all his ceremonial, all his occult powers, Pasqually scored a failure, and the Master who emerged from the unseen, carrying such high ascribed warrants, permitted himself, through sheer lack in resources, to be circumvented by as the emissaries of Robespierre." Meanwhile the star of Saint-Martin's influence grew from more to more. *L'Homme de Desir* was reprinted several times, and in the highest circles of society, at Strasbourg and Paris, in the palace of the Duchesse de Bourbon, amidst the convulsions of the revolutions he taught the way of the mystics.

LATER LIFE AND WRITINGS

It was at Strasbourg and, I think, towards the end of his sojourn in this city of blessed memories that Saint-Martin wrote another of his most suggestive treatises, *Le Nouvel Homme*, "the aim of which," as he tells us, "is to describe what we should expect in regeneration." It presents three epochs of symbolism: the first corresponds to the history of Israel, regarded as that of universal election, man's own nature being the Promised Land, whence it is necessary to cast out the wicked and idolatrous nations that have ruled therein, after which the altars of the Lord must be set up instead and the Law proclaimed by the higher part of our nature. The second epoch is that of the Christ-Life, which must be conceived and born within us for the work of our redemption. All stages of the Divine Life in Palestine are marshaled to illustrate the story of the *New Man* from the moment of His birth within us to that of mystical death, and from the descent into the underworld to the last and greatest mystery on the Mountain of Ascension. To the Second Advent belongs the third epoch of symbolism, being that of the Apocalypse, the new heaven and the new earth declared within us, the tabernacle of God with men, the Celestial Jerusalem built up into our spiritual being.

The sojourn at Strasbourg came to an end in 1791, and for perhaps a year Saint-Martin was chiefly at Paris, where he wrote his neat book, entitled *Ecce Homo*; "to forewarn people against the wonders and prophecies of the time," to indicate the "degree of abasement" into which man has fallen and of which the passion for lower marvels, like those of somnambulism, appears to be the prime example. The thesis in this sense is a strange but pregnant commentary respecting the transmutation of interests on the part of one who for a moment was integrated in a school of Mesmer and was a friend or fellow-worker of Puysegur. *Ecce Homo* was partly written as a counsel for the Duchesse de Bourbon and very likely in her own house. It appeared prior to *Le Nouvel Homme*, though composed subsequently: both worlds, however, were published in 1792, the Reign of Terror notwithstanding. Saint-Martin was still in Paris during a dreadful ordeal. "The streets near the house I was in were a field of battle; the house itself was a hospital where the wounded were brought and, moreover, was threatened every moment with invasion and pillage. In the midst of all this I had to go, at the risk of my life, to take care of my sister, half a league from my dwelling." It is to be inferred from a later record that the "dwelling" was that of the Duchesse.

There is no space here to speak of Saint-Martin's political theories, of his feelings towards the French Revolution, of certain things without importance or consequence which occurred to him therein. I am concerned only with the deeper issues of his life and thoughts. A writer on errors and truths had obviously something to say on the basis of governments, the authority of sovereigns and on jurisprudence, while a searcher of religion and theosophy, who had passed through the world-crisis at the end of the eighteenth century at its very heart and center, could neither fail to have his part therein nor to leave us reflections thereon. We have *Philosophical and Religious Considerations on the French Revolution, Light on Human Association* and a few other pamphlets which do not call to be named.

Saint-Martin also had some activities of another kind imposed upon him, such as, e.g., when he was called to the Ecole Normale, instituted to train teachers for public instruction. These things did not last and left no mark behind them. In September 1792, the health of his father called him again to Amboise, where he remained for a year, or a considerable time after the father's death. We hear of him then at Petit Bourg, a country house of the Duchesse de Bourbon, and afterwards at Paris till the spring of 1794, when "a decree against the privileged and proscribed classes, amongst which it was his lot to be born, enforced his return to Amboise till it was canceled in his respect in January, 1795, when the work of L'Ecole Normale brought him back to the capital for a period. His time appears to have been divided between Paris and his native town till the end of 1799, and I mention this year because on December 24 Saint-Martin lost so much by the death of the Baron Kirchberger de Liebistorf, a kindred spirit with whom he had maintained for five years what I described long ago as "the most memorable, the most beautiful, the most fascinating of all theosophical correspondences." It became available in English so far back as 1863, but the edition has been out of print for decades, and I question whether there could be a better gift than an annotated translation at the present day by one who knows Saint-Martin, his work and has period. It contains the true marrow, spirit, and quintessence of the French mystic, and has been referred to often in my notes.

His devotion to Jacob Bohme was the chief mental characteristic of his later life; it is ever present in his correspondences above described, but I have never been able to see that it changed his own views: it may be true to say that it deepened them, but he was on sure mystic ground already before the Teutonic theosopher gave him has own light.

I do not think that it would have helped him to alter for the better one line of *L'Homme de Desir*, though he has left it on record that in the light of Jacob Bohme he should have written *Le Nouvel Homme* differently, or perhaps not at all. In the year 1800 *L'Esprit des Choses* appeared at Paris in two volumes, with a Latin epigraph on the title in which it was affirmed that "man is the mirror of the totality of things." Concerning this suggestive work Saint-Martin has offered three points of information: That it was projected originally under the title of Natural Revelations, collected from original notes, with additions thereunto; that it embraces the whole circle of things physical and scientific, spiritual, and Divine; that it is a kind of introduction to the works of Jacob Bohme. The last in its final reduction must be called indicative of intention, and Saint-Martin, I do not doubt, was conscious that his own intimations were in bonds of spiritual espousals with his great German peer, but in their contributions to the higher literature of the soul there are no two mystics so utterly unlike each other in all their former and modes. It is a question, therefore, of penetrating below the surface, when that which we reach is the heart of union common to all who have followed the great quest of experience in God. It is certain that Saint-Martin grew daily in the consciousness of such union with Boehm, and when he continued in his own manner to deliver his own message it seemed to him doubtless that he was following the message of his precursor. For *L'Esprit des Choses*, man is the organ of Divine Order, man is the mirror of all things. Nature is in somnambulism, and we are involved therein, whence I suppose it may be inferred. that she waits on our awaking and passes out of sleep in us. These things and many others are notions which were with Saint-Martin from the beginning. Occasionally there are higher and deeper things than those which we have heard previously, but they are not of Bohme nor of any other than the French mystic himself — as, e.g., that the soul becomes the Name of the Lord, and the Name is declared within it.

There are practically no materials for the external life of Saint- Martin after the year 1799; the *Portrait Historique* tells us practically nothing, and we know of him only from his books. In the closing years of his life, he was working zealously at translations of Bohme, Aurora, *The Three Principles, Forty Questions* and *Threefold Idle of Man*, but he. had made a beginning much earlier. We are not concerned with these versions, but *Le Ministere de l'Homme-Esprit*, published in 1802, his last original work, is in some respects the most important of all and from his own-point of view was written more clearly than the rest, though he felt its remoteness from common human notions and human interests It has been held to illustrate his intention of marrying his "first school" to the Teutonic theosopher, but again the kind of marriage is that of the amity at the root of all the great mystics and their great subjects. For the rest, the book is built based on his own anterior writings, the substance of which he presents in the opening pages, as he also gives a summary of Bohme and indicates unawares certain salient points of doctrinal correspondence between the latter and Martines de Pasqually exhibited in *La Reintegration des Etres*. Apart from all systems and all authorities, the ministry is a book of innumerable detached lights, some of which belong to the order of first magnitude. It is possible to name only its "intimations of immortality," of death and the gate of life, of the path which is opened in regeneration, of spiritual life and its communication, of the Sabbath attained by Nature, the Sabbath of the soul and the Sabbath of the Word. There is also the doctrine of the Eternal Word, as it passed through the alembic of the French mystic's mind, its relation to the universe and man, how it is the measure of all things and is the very Word of Life, in opposition to that which Saint-Martin calls the Word of Death.

The Ministry has been termed his swan's song, but it is rather his last contemplation, in which he opened many wells of thought and looked across many paths of vision. On January 18, 1803, he recorded in his notes that this date completed his sixtieth year and that it had opened to him a new world. "My spiritual hopes proceed in growth continual. I advance, thanks be to God, towards those great beatitudes which were shown forth to me long ago and shall crown all joys with which I have been encompassed continually in my, earthly life." A note added in the summer says that he had received certain warnings of a physical enemy and thought that it would carry him of as it had done with his father before him. He asked only the help of Providence, that he might hold himself prepared for the event. On October 13, 1803, at Aulnay, near Sceaux, in the house of a friend – Comte Lenoir La-Roche – after an apoplectic stroke, he passed painlessly away in a final act of prayer.

MODERN MARTINISM

It will be seen that I have depended throughout on printed documents, no others being available to research in England, but that the sources of many which have been quoted are in the archives of the Martinist Order. They would appear to form, however, comparatively a small part of those which have been certified as extant at different periods. We are told that the archives of the Elect Priesthood were deposited in 1781 with Savalette de Langes, who was the President of the Philalethes; that after his death they were sold indiscriminately, together with those of the Philalethes and the Rite Ecossais Philosophique, and were purchased for next to nothing by three Masonic Brethren, who returned them to the proper quarters, two of them retaining these of the Elect Priesthood, as they had been members of the Rite; that this restitution took place in 1806; that the two custodians delivered them in 1809 to another member, named Destigny, on his return from St. Domingo,. he being a legatee of Pasqually, and having otherwise a greater claim upon them; that Destigny was already in possession of the surviving West Indian archives; that in 1812 his collection was enriched by those of the Orient of Avignon, which had been taken into Italy prior to the Revolution; that the whole remained in his keeping till 1868, when he transferred them to M. Villarial, a year before his death, in whose possession they continued at least till the end of 1899. They comprised the records of eleven Orients - otherwise Lodges — of the Order, those of Leogana in the West Indies having been lost in a fire, and those of Lyons having come into the hands of Papus otherwise of the Martinist Order.

As regards the archives of Lyons we are told by Papus whence and how they or their transcripts were derived by him. His account has been summarized in my second chapter. I have specified also the documents in the hands of M. Matter's descendants, he being himself a descendant of Rodolphe de Salzmann, whom I have mentioned previously as one of the Strasbourg circle. They are said to include the correspondence of Saint-Martin with Salzmann himself, with Mme de Boecklin, the Comte de Divonne. and others, as also that of Salzmann. But there are owners of other collections D'Effinger, Toumyer, Munier — who are not even names to us. Of each and all it has to be said that nothing has been heard from them for over twenty years and that the Great War has intervened. We have been promised for the same period a *Histoire Generale de l'Ordre des Elus Coens* and a study of Willermoz based on the archives of Lyons, but they have not appeared, and we are not likely to see them. In view of the wealth of material it may well be that the definitive life of Saint-Martin and of has earlier if not later concerns still remain to be done. I have presented a mere outline, and in some sense a supplement to my former extended work.

It remains to speak briefly of L'Ordre Martiniste. We learn from Camille Flammarion that between 1860 and 1870 he was acquainted with a litterateur named Henri Delaage, who is mentioned also by Eliphas Levi; that he heard much from Delaage concerning M. de Chaptal, his grandfather, who knew Saint-Martin, apparently fairly well. These are the bare facts, to which it may be added that at the beginning of his occult life Papus seemingly got to know Delaage and received from him, some months before the latter's death, what is termed a *pauvre depot, constitue par deux lettres et quelques* points in fact, the modern Martinist cipher S I which is rendered Silencieux Inconnus, otherwise the Unknown Silent Ones. Delaage had written in his time two or three occult books which were fantastic in matter and impossible in style. They do not suggest his connection with any society for the exposition of Saint-Martin's mystical teaching, either secretly or in public, and so far as Papus is concerned he fails to explain why the cipher was communicated or what it signified to the previous custodian. It led him, however, to believe and proclaim in terms of certitude that Saint-Martin had himself initiated M. de Chaptal and to establish or reconstitute L'Ordre Martintiste in 1884. Between 1887 and 1890 he produced Rituals for the Order, arranged in three Degrees, which I have praised on several occasions for their sincerity, simplicity, and reserve in respect of claims. They were termed Associate, Initiated Martinist, and Initiator, the last implied by its title — conveying a license for the propagation of the Order by all who had attained this its highest rank. Every person who held the Third Degree could thus constitute a new center.

The mode adopted was usually that which is known technically as "communication," that is to say, personally and not in Lodge or Temple. To my certain knowledge reception was arranged even by post. It is obvious that after this manner a vast membership could be secured in a very short space, assuming any reasonable zeal among the workers and something colorable or attractive on which they could act. Moreover, there were no fees of any kind. There is no question that L'Ordre Martiniste spread rapidly in France, and in addition to the delegates constituted automatically by the Third Degree there were Lodges in various towns. There was membership also in other countries, England itself not excepted, while the Order was especially successful in North and South America. We hear also of propagation in Egypt and even Asia.

In 1891 a Supreme Council was constituted in Paris and ruled the whole Order. It became a center also for numerous collateral interests, all carefully organized, including esoteric groups and Faculties of Science and Philosophy, which held examinations apparently and granted degrees at their value. Papus was an indefatigable worker, and before the century was out it must be acknowledged that he was at the head of a movement which may be almost called colossal in respect of its magnitude. The reasons are not far to seek it was a form of initiation and it made no claim on Masonry; it received both sexes; it had a distinct religious side, apart from dogmatism and — outside all sectarianism it was in some sense a Christian thing. As such, it must have appealed to multitudes in France who had lost faith in the Latin Church and yet had spiritual interests. Moreover, it carried the seals and talismans of occult sciences, which it claimed' to teach and to reconcile with the regnant science of the day. As such, its apparent justifications, if not its warrants, were in Spiritism, Psychical Research, the Schools of Nancy and Salpetriere not to speak of the less recognized though not less momentous school of Animal Magnetism. But having offered this appreciation I have virtually set L'Ordre Martiniste at the poles asunder from Saint-Martin the mystic. In late and early writings Papus affirmed continually that when the disciple of Pasqually followed his own path, having left that of his Master, he not only established a Masonic Rite, as others had said previously, but also an Order of his own which spread even into Russia. Now, his so-called evidence is out of court in every case. I have examined them long since and set them utterly aside: there is no need to retrace the ground. The Masonic historians were blundering over terms and titles when they foisted a Rite on Saint-Martin, and Papus was reading in a glass of vision whence saw the mystic at the head of an Order propagated like his own. I leave it at this, though it is difficult to understand how he could have deceived himself. He has not escaped criticism of a rougher kind, but to me it seems that he had a constitutional incapacity for pronouncing validly on questions of evidence and that anything passed for proof in respect to his own bias.

The fact remains that in 1899 or thereabouts L'Ordre Martiniste may be said to have reached its zenith, but it had sown, I think, already the seeds of its own destruction. It had begun to encroach on the Masonic field and was approaching perilously the position of an unauthorized aspect of the Craft. Practically the entire branch of the Order in North America, extending to thousands, broke away from the Supreme Council at Paris and reincorporated independently on this account alone. A few only continued under the old obedience, among others the novelist Margaret B. Peeke, who was rewarded by Papus with the Grade of Rose Croix. There are no statistics before me, but it seems certain that in France — where Freemasonry, such as it is, must be called exceedingly strong the course taken could have been scarcely less than disastrous; yet it was not amended in consequence. The years went on, and I think that L'Initiation, an official Martinist publication, came to an end before the War. But the Great War came, which broke up everything belonging to occult interests of the organized kind. The Grand Master Papus died in the course of it, in the heroism of a physician's service. The peace of Versailles was at last signed, and at no long time thereafter the old interests began to lift up their heads: it seemed also as if the relapsed tension itself gave birth automatically to new adventures by the score in thought and dream.

Occultism in Paris was characterized by activities of every kind – new movements, new associations, new periodicals, including many official organs for one or another dedication, but most of them mushroom growths. We can imagine that L'Ordre Martiniste did not remain in abeyance, but it seems now a shadow of its former self, is split up by rival obedience's and has entered into union with decried Masonic Rites. Whether it will emerge into clearer light no one remote from the center can dare to say, but to all appearances at least its time is over. Once at the head of most French movements of the occult kind, it is now but one of a score; and I do not know in what sense the gracious spirit of Saint-Martin can be said to abide therein. If ever a time shall come when those who move in its circle and those who rule at its center will have realized that he left for ever the occult and Masonic sanctuaries for the Church Mystic of Christian Theosophy, they may find his directing light shining towards the end of true Mysticism; but in the Orients of Memphis never, and never in those of Mizraim, or in any substituted form of Freemasonry which is without God in the world. Meanwhile I tend to believe that men and women of spiritual mind in France, who are not under the obedience of Rome, will remember Saint-Martin as one who after his own manner belongs to that great chain which began in the Christian world with Dionysus the Areopagite and added link to link through all the ages subsequent.

Pillars of the Temple

Let the Student recall in the first place his experience with two figurative Pillars in the Craft Grades of Masonry, how the significance of one is explained to him at the beginning of his life of brotherhood, and that of the second at the next stage of his progress. The importance attributed to both is of that kind precisely which would lead him to expect that he might hear further and more definitely concerning them in some later grade of his advancement. Such, however, is not the case: they pass out of sight completely and he is left at a loose end, wondering perhaps why they have been introduced to his notice in this very express manner, or — with a better gift of reflection — concluding tentatively that he may be said to stand between them as on the threshold of the Master Grade and to issue between them into that Temple built of old, about which he hears in the central legend of the Craft. He has otherwise finished with them forever, not only within the measures of the Craft but in the several sequences of High Grades which are in general knowledge and activity among us. We meet with this kind of inconsequence in all the Ritual Departments. A curtain is drawn for a moment upon a prospect which looks practicable, but it falls again suddenly, and the Candidate does not enter therein. It is as if something were proposed in the mind of makers of Ritual from which they were diverted afterwards, leaving their design unfinished.

Hiram, The Widow's Son

Now, the source of the symbolism is I Kings vii. 13-22, the artificer concerned being Hiram, described as "a widow's son of the tribe of Naphtali," whom Solomon sent and fetched out of Tyre. "He cast two Pillars of brass; eighteen cubits high each.... And he made two chapiters of molten brass, to set upon the tops of the Pillars: the height of the one chapiter was five cubits, and the height of the other chapiter was five cubits. And nets of checker work and wreaths of chain work, for the chapiters.... And two rows..... to cover the chapiters.... with pomegranates.... And the chapiters... were of lily work.... And he set up the Pillars in the Porch of the Temple: and he set up the right Pillar and called the name thereof Jachin: and he set lip the left Pillar and called the name thereof Boaz.... So was the work of the Pillars finished" See also 2 Chronicles iii. 15-17.

JACHIN AND BOAZ

On this text the Kabalistic treatise, entitled *Gates of Light*, comments as follows: "He who knows the mysteries of the two Pillars, which are Jachin and Boaz, shall understand after what manner the Neshamoth, or Minds, descend with the Ruachoth, or Spirits, and the Nephasoth, or Souls, through El-chai and Adonai by the influx of the said two Pillars." It is an allegory of the descent of spiritual man from the Supernal World into Malkuth, the kingdom of this world, which apart from human intelligence is said to be void "even as the poor man who possesses nothing." It is said, also, that because of this descent there shall be built the city of Zion, which is Jerusalem — that is to say, a spiritual city, a house not made with hands, such as Masons are held to build in their hearts. In the Kabalistic Tree of Life, Chokmah and Binah are the entablatures of the two Pillars, Chesed and Geburah are the chapiters, while the bodies of the Pillars represent Netzach and Hod. "By these two Pillars and by El-chai the Minds and Spirits and Souls descend, as by their passages or channels."

Parts of the Soul

It should be understood that Neshama = Mind and is the superior grade of the soul in man; Ruach = Spirit and is the rational faculty; and Nephesh = Soul and is *anima vivens et vitalis*, i.e., sensitive life. The reference is not therefore to three classes of spiritual being, but to three aspects of individual human life. El-chai signifies Living God and is that title of Divinity which relates to Yesod. The meaning of the word Jachin is indicated in the commentary to represent that power which establishes or imprints form upon the formless and is understood especially of the formation of man and his members, whence it is said, in Deuteronomy xxxii. 6: "Hath He not made thee and formed thee?" The significance of Boaz is to be sought in PSALM lxviii. 35: "He that giveth strength and power," because Boaz receives its strength from Geburah and its vigor from Binah. As regards the two Pillars taken conjointly, they are connected with the Song of Solomon v.15: "His legs are as pillars of marble, set upon sockets of fine gold." It is affirmed finally that "whosoever advances in the study of the Written and Oral Laws.... unites the Blessed Name and the mystery of Jachin and Boaz."

The Secret of Israel

The mind of Israel has been always the mind of the Mysteries, and the secret of Israel is also a secret of initiation. It is for this reason — as I think — that Jewry produced Christianity, even as the city of this world is the material of the Mystic City. If we take in succession the symbolical stages through which a Masonic Candidate advances in the course of his progress through the authentic Rites and Grades, we shall find that farther light concerning them is derivable from Kabalistic literature, and especially from that vast work which

I have named under the title of Zohar, together with its supplements and dependencies.

The Kabalistic system of theosophy proposes Four Worlds, those of pure Deity, of Creation, Formation and of things material and infra-material — understood as the World of Action and its recrement. Each of these worlds is comprised in the conventional scheme, which is called the Tree of Life, though it includes three Pillars, which are those of Wisdom, Strength, and Beauty, though they are usually misplaced in Masonry. That on the right — as an observer faces the Tree — is termed the Pillar of Mercy; on the left is the Pillar of Severity, and in the middle that of Benignity. Above is the World of Deity. Through these Pillars, as by paths leading to an Eternal Sanctuary, the soul is supposed to pass till it reaches the Divine End. But that which returns to the Divine is that also which came forth therefrom infra-material as the conception of emanation assumes — and this theosophy suggests that the divine and intellectual principles which constitute the complete man descended or were evolved through the Pillar of Mercy, to be manifested at the end of the emanation in that which is termed the Kingdom, being this present external world. Through the Pillar of Severity, the written and oral law — or the Jewish Scriptures and their secret explanation — are supposed to have descended in their turn and to have been manifested ultimately on this earth. The redemption of humanity takes place through the Pillar of Benignity, signifying that the soul enters salvation by going back on the paths which it has travelled. This scheme recalls the great parable of Pausanias concerning the Grades of Venus. The Tree of Life signifies the mystery of man's origin and his return whence he came.

A Way of Going Back

The true method of that return is and can be the only field of research which is covered by the real Mysteries. It is the chief subject of Kabalism, and some reflections therefrom are found in Masonic Ritual. I do not suggest that Masonry is a qualified Kabalism; crudities of this kind are offences of a bygone day; but it is substantially certain that the anonymous craftsmen who elaborated the Craft Degrees had some vestiges of knowledge concerning the theosophy evolved in Jewry outside the Law and the Prophets.

London Morning Post's Attack on Freemasonry

For Seventeen Days in succession, ending July 30, *The Morning Post* published a remarkable series of articles on "The Cause of World Unrest," the work of two anonymous writers, with occasional intervention on the part of leading articles, generalizing on the subjects treated, and of occasional correspondents, chief among whom is Mrs. Nesta H. Webster, author of a book issued in 1919 under the title of The French Revolution. As expressed in a short announcement of July 12, the articles claim to disclose "the existence of a revolutionary movement in which Jews and secret societies play a leading part."

On July 24, another announcement stated that "thousands of new readers have been taking *The Morning Post* during the publication of the series." Accepting this implicitly on the honorable assurance of the oldest morning paper, I regard it as incumbent on myself to review the whole question, in so far as it affects the things for which I stand and the dedications of my literary life. The nature of the secret societies incriminated emerges in another passage which appeared on July 21 and affirmed that for a long period of time a conspiracy has been gradually developing for the overthrowing of the existing Christian form of civilization; that the prime agents of this conspiracy are Jews and revolutionary Freemasons; and that its object "is to pave the way for the world supremacy of a chosen people." I propose on my part to show that the writers are utterly misinformed, where it is possible for an individual critic to cheek them, and that it would be curious therefore — as well as difficult to suppose — if they are mainly or substantially correct over their findings in those political realms which lie beyond my field of research.

It is to be observed that the existence of a plot for "the destruction of all Christian Empires, Altars and Thrones" is an old Roman Catholic thesis, put forward long prior to the War. One of the forms which it took was a review of the Dreyfus case, and it not only made common cause of the Latin Church against Freemasonry, but seems to have been part of that cause. A periodical, called *La Revue des Societes Secretes*, was filled with the case against Freemasonry and the case against Israel. The management of both issues was of similar value, being the enumeration and repetition of various less or more familiar facts on which a false construction was placed, or of statements that were probably untrue. Both forms being equally effective in impressing those who were unversed, the first was pursued when possible. My thesis is that the revelations in The Morning Post on "the cause of world unrest," the "most formidable sect in the world" and "the terror in France," but especially on "the red curtain in Freemasonry," the *"arriere Loges"* and the "ritual of revenge" bear all the marks and signs of derivation from the same mint, appeal to the same sources, and are speaking the same language as the French anti-Masonry of the last thirty years and over. They are the work of writers belonging to the Latin Church or alternatively content to depend — so far as Freemasonry is concerned — solely on material which, during the period specified, has been dished up in various forms for the one purpose with which Rome is concerned on this side of its activity — namely, the forlorn hope of destroying the "iniquitous sect" of Masonry, and presumably to maintain at white heat the old hostility of France to Jewry and all connoted thereby. I speak with a certain authority, for it happens that I know the leading literature of anti-Masonry, on what it has depended on from the beginning, and the contentions which it will sustain to the end. It happens also that I am a Freemason, holding the chief Rites and Degrees, under one or other obedience, that I know the literature of Freemasonry, its history *ab origine symboli* and the great cloud of its rituals. If I flourish, for once in my life, a trumpet of this kind, it is in order that the anti-Masonic sect, wheresoever dispersed over the world, in whichever of its disguises, and in this or that of its regular, or casual journals, may learn exactly where they are. Finally, I am a Christian and Catholic Mystic, and by Catholicism embraces all that belongs to the eternal in the symbolism of Roman Doctrine and Ritual. It comes about in this manner, that for me Emblematic Freemasonry is a Mystery of the relations between God, Man, and the Universe, set forth in the figurative and sacramental forms of sacred ceremonial. It will be understood on this basis that those various associations which, in France and other Latin countries, while still wearing an outward guise of Freemasonry, regard the belief in God and immortality, the intercourse between God and the soul represented by the Bible and other Sacred Books as matters of personal opinion — to be held or not according to mental predilection — have made void their Masonic titles. They are cut off from communion with the vital and spiritual source: they may be political or not, revolutionary or not, monarchical and otherwise "reactionary," or the reverse of these; they are in no case part of my concern. The question is whether the writers in *The Morning Post* have followed a line of accusation which incriminates all Freemasonry even when it offers a distinction; and the answer is that they have. Out of this there arises the further question whether they and the Roman Catholic crusaders, on whom they depend, are competent witnesses on the Masonic side of their subject; and the answer is that they are not.

It is obvious and goes without saying that the articles are not written by Masons holding under any obedience, and my thesis is that they betray the most extraordinary ignorance on elementary matters respecting the Craft and its developments.

London Morning Post's Attack on Freemasonry

It is recognized from the beginning that English Freemasonry is not to be included by their sweeping thesis concerning universal revolution, but it is affirmed that "there is Freemasonry and Freemasonry." More correctly there is Freemasonry and there are things which masquerade in its likeness but do not belong thereto. Anyone acquainted with the subject would know that true Freemasonry is neither English nor English-speaking only, neither British, Colonial nor American, to the exclusion of other countries. It is certain that prior to the War Germanic Freemasonry had no poisoned wells of political concern. There are also other countries — and I should place Sweden among them — where "pure and ancient Freemasonry," with some flowers of its later development, are equally uncontaminated as to root and branch and blossom. But having made the distinction in question, like a proverbial sop to Cerberus, the articles proceed to garner some time-immemorial charges of French origin against Templar Freemasonry and the Scottish Rite as one of its custodians, which is a charge against English as well as continental bodies. The writers seem unaware that there are great Templar jurisdictions in England, Scotland, and Ireland, and Supreme Councils of the Thirty-Third Degree. I have said therefore that their line of accusation incriminates all Freemasonry, even when it claims to do otherwise. It is not that there is "malice afore-thought," of which I find no signs; but the writers have entered a field which calls for special knowledge, and they have not even a smattering. They affirm, for example, that there are at least thirty-three degrees of Masonry, whereas there are fourteen hundred in the historical list of Ragon, and over two hundred less or more in activity at the present day.

It is impossible within the limits of this study to enumerate all the misconceptions, but the following examples may stand for the whole. To illustrate an alleged vengeance formula in the Craft rituals, it is said that the candidate for the grade of Master hears for the first time of a murdered founder, whose fate has to be avenged. This is erroneous. The legend is concerned with an assassination which is represented as duly expiated in the order of law and justice. There is no *arriere pensee* and there is no consequence in the life of Craft Masonry. It will be seen that this invention inculpates English Masonry as associated with a vendetta which is foisted on Masonry abroad. It is said correctly that there is the quest of a Lost Word in Masonry, which Word is arbitrarily affirmed to be Jehovah, and explained — with unthinkable logic — to signify natural religion. There is no such meaning tolerated by the orthodox Grades. There are various Sacred Names, carrying their proper philological import; in branches of Masonry belonging to the symbolical time of the Old Covenant they are derived for the most part from the Old Testament; but in those which belong to the New and Eternal Covenant the Name is Christ. The last misconception which I shall notice among points of ritual and symbolism is the folly that terms the Craft degrees Jewish, thus implicitly connecting them — under all their obedience, English and continental — with an alleged Jewish peril. It is obvious that allegories dealing with Solomon's Temple must contain Jewish material in the nature of things. The imbecility is to draw any inference therefrom as to the work of Jews in Masonry. Even "the Word of God" is Jewish in the Old Testament, yet I fail to see that the circulation of the Scriptures is playing into the hands of Israel, in order that it may possess the world. The Craft rituals as we have them are the work of Christian hands, Protestant enough in all conscience and therefore suspect by Rome; but Jewry had no share therein.

Passing now from ceremonial questions to matters of external fact, it is affirmed that Philippe Egalite, Duc d'Orleans, was not only Grand Master of the Grand Orient — a creation, by the way, of 1773 — but of the Templars also. Now, it so happens that The Morning Post does not know what it means when it speaks of Templar grades. There was something like six Rites incorporating this element, all independent in origin, working and history. Philippe Egalite stood at the head of none. The only purely Templar Rite in France during his reign as Master was the Strict Observance, the titular patron of which was in Germany, not in France where a Lyonnese merchant, named J.B. Willermoz, was Provincial Grand Master of Auvergne. A certain Council of Emperors possessed the Templar Kadosh Grade, but it was not a Templar Rite. Philippe Egalite took such an active interest in Masonry and had so great a faith in its possibilities that when he was elected Grand Master in 1771 his presence could be hardly secured for installation; and he exhibited the uttermost negligence in that capacity, while in 1793 he repudiated Freemasonry in the Journal de Paris. He affirmed that it had once presented to his mind "an image of equality," but that he had found the reality and so left the phantom. He was further of the opinion that there should be no mystery and no secret assembly in a republic. The Grand Orient declared the headship vacant and a few months later the guillotine closed the question so far as the quondam Grand Master was concerned. These are the facts, with which we may compare the long since exploded fictions reproduced by *The Morning Post* on the subject of Philippe Egalite engineering his vast machine of Masonry to consummate revolution.

It is affirmed that Frederick the Great of Prussia was Grand Master of a world-wide system of Freemasonry. He was nothing of the kind. Masonic historians would take a natural pride in giving such a celebrated, if not illustrious, personality an important position in the Order; but the most that can be shown is that he was President of the Grand Lodge of the Three Globes at Berlin, his correspondence with which remains to exhibit how far away the connection was. The old, old story of the old false charter which represents him creating a Supreme

Council of the Scottish Rite as a system of Thirty-three degrees is put forward as an historical fact, but it has been abandoned long since by Masonic scholarship worthy of the name. Reflecting here as elsewhere the parti pris of Abbe Burruel, the Lodge of Les Amis Reunis and the Rite of the Philalethes are represented as *arrieres Loges* in which the Revolution was plotted. They were an open lodge and an open Rite existing in the face of day. The account is otherwise muddled, representing Savlette de Langes as belonging to the former and not the latter whereas he belonged to both, and was so much the moving spirit of the second that it is supposed to have suspended its labors when he died. As a matter of fact, the Rite was founded within the bosom of the lodge, and the Convention of Paris, held in 1784, indicates at full length the real nature of its concerns. Fortunately, the chief documents on which Burruel relies for his foolish account are in my possession: they are concerned with the occult sciences, not with Revolution.

There is another and to me more important matter. The great French mystic, Louis Claude de Saint-Martin, is represented as a political "fanatic" and a member of the alleged revolutionary lodges. This is partly on the authority of Barruel and partly on that of a converted Jew, named Lemann, who became a Roman Catholic priest. The latter affirms that Saint-Martin "developed" the "sect" of Pasqually after the latter's death. I cast back the statements into the mouths of their makers. The French mystic had no sect, no Rite, though he had a great number of unincorporated disciples. He did not belong to the Rite of the Philalethes or Les Amis Reunis. He became a Mason in his youth but left the Order to follow "the inward way." I appeal to my Life of Louis Claude de Saint-Martin, published in 1900. As regards Martines de Pasqually — whose very name is blundered, still following Barruel — *The Morning Post* affirms that he "worked in France on very much the same lines as Weishaupt," founder of the Illuminati, "worked in Germany." In reply to this amazing rubbish, I appeal to the same work of twenty years since and need only add here that in such case Weishaupt worked in "occult communications" by virtue of which it was supposed that — the Christ of Palestine instructed the Brethren of Pasqually's Masonic Rite of Elect Priests — *Rit des Elus Cohens* — according to that which was called in their terminology *la voie sensible*. It is a new view of the German revolution-manger, and *The Morning Post* will find that "second thoughts are best." As against some other misstatements of Lemann and Abbe Barruel, Pasqually was not a Jew. He was born in the parish of Notre Dame (Saint-Hugues), town and diocese of Grenoble. The baptism of one of his children on June 20, 1768, is on record in the municipal archives of Bordeaux. In or about the year 1780 that brilliant adventurer who called himself Count Cagliostro, founded a Rite of Egyptian Masonry, which filled for a brief period the Masonic world of France with wonder. This is also garnered by *The Morning Post* into its indiscriminate net of revolution-plots. There could be nothing more antecedently ridiculous, and again it happens that the rituals are in my possession, while I am acquainted otherwise at first hand with the written laws and constitutions. Egyptian Masonry was an occult Rite, belonging to Hermetic Masonry and more especially designed to sustain the claims of Cagliostro as possessing the Great Secret of the Universal Medicine. I observe that the author of the article under notice identifies the "Grand Copht" with Joseph Balsamo, so he has not read the evidence against this view produced by Mr. W. R. Trowbridge, who is not a Mason and has no job in Romanism or revolution questions.

After this enumeration there remain over three matters which deserve studies set apart to each. I have indicated a root-opinion on the part of *The Morning Post* that the Templar Movement in Masonry is contained within the measures of a single system, being in fact the Scottish Rite — a somewhat inchoate collection of thirty high grades superposed on those of the Craft. It is a development from that Council of Emperors, which superposed twenty-two Grades, and as regards both they are not Templar Rites in the proper sense of the words. The Rite of the Strict Observance was solely and militantly Templar, *ab origine symboli*. It superposed three Grades, of which the first — or Master of St. Andrew's — formed a connecting link between the Craft and two exceedingly important modes of Templar chivalry. It used to be said that it was Jacobite at the inception but was certainly not. Here for the first time — albeit by implication only — it is accused of political purpose, under the Duke of Brunswick. As a fact the writer in *The Morning Post* does not know that he is impeaching the Strict Observance: he seems to think in his state of confusion that the Duke of Brunswick was "Grand Master of the German Freemasons" because he was Grand Master of certain Ecossais lodges. As regards the Scottish Rite — *Antiquos Scoticus Ritus Acceptus*, as it is called in the forged Constitutions — it did not come into existence till 1801, and then at Charleston, U.S.A. In this connection the articles remind us that Stephen Morin carried a warrant from Grand Consistory of Masons, countersigned by the Grand Orient, to America, and there began to confer high grade powers on a number of Jews, among them Hippolyto Joseph Da Costa, who was not a Jew at all, and at a subsequent date Would have died in the hands of the Holy Inquisition at Lisbon, if he had not been rescued by English Masons, facts perhaps naturally omitted by writers in *The Morning Post*. So much for Morin. We hear also in 1801 of the first Supreme Council in Charleston when Jews were again prominent, among them being Frederick Dalcho. Our contemporary is unfortunate, for Dalcho, who was of Prussian origin and English birth, was for twenty-two years a priest of the American Episcopal Church, and a monument to his memory is still standing in the vestry of St. Michael's at Charleston.

These are the kind of qualifications which pronounce on "Red Masonry" and presume to talk of revolution in connection with the Scottish Rite. The same fatal blundering pursues the articles when they proceed to Albert Pike and his work in the Southern Jurisdiction of that obedience. The writer is of course unaware that Pike reconstructed the rituals and that they stand therefore at his value as a symbolist and critical scholar: the value is unfortunately very slight. But those who suggest that he imported revolutionary notions into his Masonic Order are talkers of rank nonsense, and the quotation from his *Morals and Dogma* which is made in Article IV, on the profanation of Masonry by plotters of anarchy — whatever its value as history — is sufficient as to his own position. Among the evidence offered to the contrary are ritual counsels to destroy Ignorance, Tyranny and Fanaticism. Very well: be it agreed that this is part of the design of Masonry. Does *The Morning Post* stand for ignorance, stand for Tyranny, and stand for Fanaticism? No; but Roman Anti-Masonry — which it reflects throughout the Masonic part of these articles — invariably regards every plan for their removal as a siege laid against the walls of its Spiritual City. As one who knows all the rituals of the Scottish Rite and has made a long critical study of many codices of each, I am able to check wild statements respecting their content. For example, I am familiar with some twenty separate and independent versions of the Rose Croix, and I affirm that Barruel lied when he said that the French ritual current at his period represents Christ as "a common Jew crucified for his crimes." I challenge *The Morning Post* and its anonymous contributors to produce any codex which does. In France then, as in England now, Christ — for the Rose Croix — is the Son of God and Lord of Glory. I lay down the same challenge respecting alleged "subversive forms of Freemasonry" working "a ritual of hatred for the Cross." Templar or non-Templar, there are no such grades. The Cross is an object of veneration in Christian Masonry, and in some of the "philosophized" degrees it is treated as a universal symbol. Now the Templar rituals were Christian in all their forms during the eighteenth century, but a few were philosophized afterwards. The Rite of the Strict Observance has been always Christian. Here again I know all its rituals, including those which are held in great secrecy. They were communicated to me after the same long delay and under the same great reserves as was done presumably in the past. They are neither of Stuart legitimacy nor of continental anarchy: they belong to things of the spirit and God known of the heart; and the Templar Order in Britain — where it is governed by Great Priory — in the Colonies and America, belongs to the same category. This notwithstanding, the claim to descend from the old Knights Templar is a myth and pure invention. *Couteulx de Canteleu* is a false witness on this subject, just as Copin Albancelli is an *hysterique insatiable* about the Jews.

I pass now to the German Order of Illuminati. It may have been observed that the root-authority on which *The Morning Post* depends for its case against Masonry is Abbe Barruel, in an almost forgotten work, entitled Memoirs of Jacobinism. He is said to trace the origin of the French Revolution through a bewildering maze of secret societies; but as a fact his societies are Masonic, plus German Illuminism, the position regarding the latter being one of extreme simplicity. The Bavarian Order of Illuminati was founded by Adam Weishaupt in 1776, and it was suppressed by the Elector of Bavaria in 1789, some of its active members and the author of its more advanced rituals having withdrawn previously. Those who say that "it was continued in more secret forms" have never produced one item of real evidence. *The Morning Post* affirms that the Illuminate came out of their seclusion and attempted a revolution in Berlin in 1918. There is again not a shadow of proof that they did anything of the kind, though a few revolutionaries of that date took over some catchwords adopted by the original gang. Weishaupt assumed in his Order the name of Spartacus, and *The Morning Post* reproduces a question raised by Mrs. Webster — namely, whether it was "mere coincidence" that the Spartacists of modern Germany "adopted the pseudonym of their fellow-countryman and predecessor of the eighteenth century." The simple and obvious answer is that it was not coincidence but imitation. Mrs. Webster is not of any importance on this part of the subject, but she has been cited often and has intervened at length in the debate. It may be well to point out that she seems to be a member of the Roman Communion, as shown by her invariable allusion to the "Catholic Church," meaning the Latin or Roman Rite. Her historical accuracy appears on August 3, when she quotes an address of Lamartine to "his fellow-Masons." Now, in that speech Lamartine mentioned expressly that he was "not a Freemason," and did not understand "the particular language" of the Order. Mrs. Webster may or may not have read the address which she cites: her evidence is not to be trusted in either case. For the rest, I can tell Mrs. Webster and all others who are concerned that the Order of Illuminate was revived in Germany to my certain knowledge about 1893; that I have all its rituals, all its Statutes, Constitutions and so forth; that it had nothing to do with politics and nothing with revolution. It follows from all the evidence that Barruel was not "justified by time" in his fantastic thesis of survival. The "formidable sect" mentioned by Mr. Winston Churchill in the House of Commons on November 5, 1919, is certainly not a succession from Adam Weishaupt. As a scheme of universal revolution German Illuminism looks formidable in the light of those archives which were published by the Bavarian Elector. So also does the Masonic Rite of Mizraim, with its Laws, Statutes and vast mass of arrangements, not to speak of the rituals representing its ninety Grades, suggest to an unfamiliar mind that it was a thing of great moment and very wide diffusion, but the cumbrous scheme never kept half-a-dozen chapters together, of all its Senates and all its Areopagite Councils. It was and remains a scheme on paper, and this is the description applying to the archives of German Illuminism, which were magnified in the mind of Barruel till they looked like a colossal conspiracy diffused everywhere. I agree with Lord Acton that the "appalling thing" is the design in matters of this kind, but in the present case it is also the thing ridiculous, for Weishaupt's House of Revolution was a house of cards, and the sands on which it was built were the parchments on which he wrote. His scheme was concealed behind the ignorance of its members, and there was no influential center to move the puppets on the external stage. There was the amiable enthusiast Baron von Knigge, who wrote up the advanced rituals and retired altogether when Weishaupt wanted to correct them.

It is gross exaggeration to suggest that the Illuminati were "in secret control of a multitude of lodges throughout Germany," for there was no such multitude in existence; it is gross exaggeration to say that Freemasons were "initiated in shoals" by von Knigge at the Convention of Wilhelmsbad in 1782. But if both statements were literal no magnitude of external membership would have made Illuminism a living reality when there was no vitality behind it. This is the general answer to the thesis of Barruel and to those who on this day have turned to his forgotten book. It also answers the question of the articles, whether the German Illuminate were the only or chief sect which had a hand in the French Revolution. It was too invertebrate from the beginning to have had a practical hand in anything, and it had passed out of existence. The mark which it left upon Masonry was in Southern Germany, where the downfall of the one Order caused the suppression of the other. All that is said about Mirabeau, his visit to Berlin and his plot to "illuminize" French Freemasonry, may be disposed of in one sentence: there is no evidence to show that Mirabeau ever became a Mason. The province of Barruel was to color everything, and he laid on the blacks and the scarlets with lavish brushes. But he was largely confined to the documents, and it is just one of those cases in which documents produce a false impression, for the reasons given.

The next point is possibly the grand divertissement of all. Those who are entitled to speak about secret societies in France at the end of the nineteenth century are aware that Leo Taxil flaunted in the face of Paris his public confession that everything concerned with Diana Vaughan, the Universal Masonic Directorium, its supreme pontificate, Lucifer in the High Grades and Le Diable au XIX Siecle, were impositions of his own invention. Everyone knows that Dr. Batame, otherwise Dr. Hacks, whose name appears as author of this work, had confessed previously, deriding the credulity of "catholics." I have always felt sure that there would be a recrudescence of these mendacities when people had forgotten the circumstances which led to their public exposure; but I did not expect it to occur in the columns of *The Morning Post*.

I have now done. On the basis of these findings, I deny that evidence has been produced for the hand of Freemasonry even in the French Revolution. The contrast made by Louis Blanc between Craft degrees for those who were to be kept in the dark and "occult lodges" for the elect is opposed by the history of French High Grades. The latter were as open to those who sought them as anything in the Craft itself. In the sense of Louis Blanc there were no occult lodges. I am sure, however, that French Freemasonry was a finger-post pointing in the direction of revolution. The Masonic watchwords of Liberty, Equality, and Fraternity were like a passing bell ringing out the old order. And the French Revolution was like the German Reformation, a pretty bad thing, but it had to come. The factory of the one was not in "shadowy sanctuaries" but in the French Court, while in the other the factory was at Rome.

The question of Co-Masonry I leave to those who are concerned. The lodges and chapters are illicit from the standpoint of the Grand Lodge of England, under whose obedience I abide as a Mason. The reasons are that it initiates women and is empowered by an irregular jurisdiction. But I believe that *The Morning Post* has discovered another mare's nest, while it is specifically wrong as usual on its points of fact. The French Lodge Libres Penseuirs did not transform into Le Droit Humain; the Order is not oriental; and its devotion to the supposed Comte de St. Germain is an incident of theosophical revelations.

As regards Latin Freemasonry in this twentieth century, I hold no brief whatever. Wheresoever dispersed over continental Europe it may be playing the game of politics, as it is said to do in South America; but there is of course no concerted effort as there is no central direction; and I have not heard a single name of importance cited in connection with the alleged doings. It would serve, I should think, no purpose for any serious government to concern itself with the scattered groups unless and until they are caught in overt acts.

I have now reviewed the whole position, and as regards "perils" and "protocols" I make no claim to know; but having spent a great part of my literary life in the criticism and exposure of fraudulent documents, one has acquired a certain instinctive — or shall I say expert? — sense on the subject. The protocols are stolen documents, presumably of French origin and therefore suspect, because in Roman Catholic circles of that country the animus against Israel has ranked second only to that against Masonry. Admittedly also there is no evidence in support of them, though they are taken on faith at their face value by both writers in *The Morning Post*. For myself I can say only that if the alleged fact of a Jewish Peril rests on no firmer ground than these documents, we may reach an *aureum saeculum redivivum* before a universal social cataclysm. For me they are not suspect; they take their place in the class to which I have referred. I shall believe in the protocols and their Elders of Israel when I believe in the Charter of Cologne, the Charter of Larmenius, and the Ecossais Constitution of Frederick the Great.

UNIVERSAL CO-FREEMASONRY

UNIVERSAL CO-FREEMASONRY

THE STORY of *La Maconnerie Mixte* in Great Britain and other English-speaking countries is merged in modern Theosophy. It migrated to India and came under the influence of Annie Besant at Benares, where the Dharma Lodge, No. 101, was founded, to be followed in due course by other Lodges at Bombay, Adyar and East Rangoon. *La Maconnerie Mixte* was first translated into English as Joint Freemasonry and was introduced as such into Great Britain in 1902 by the "Grand Officers of the Supreme Council," who on September 26 of that year consecrated the first Lodge under the name of Human Duty, No. 6, London. Whether the Supreme Council was that of France and how a Masonic Lodge can be "consecrated" without invoking the Grand Architect of the Universe must remain open questions, so far as my own knowledge is concerned. Whosoever were concerned in later proceedings took care to provide their personal commentary on the thesis of Dr. Martin by affirming in Art. I of their "Principles" that Joint Freemasonry "asserts, in accordance with the ancient declarations of Freemasonry, the existence of a creative principle, under the title of the Great Architect of the Universe." About 1905, the English title was altered to that of Universal Co-Freemasonry in Great Britain and the British Dependencies. Maria Georges Martin was recognized presumably as President and titular head, but V. Ills. Ssr. Annie Besant, 33 degree, was not only Vice-President but "Grand Master of the Supreme Council" — possibly that of Adyar. Later on, she also became "Protectress" of the Order, so arrogating to herself the Masonic status of King Edward VII. At the present day the sign of the sisterhood has been changed and Annie Besant together with the rank and file of women in Co-Freemasonry style themselves Brothers.

DHARMA WORKING

The Ritual of the first Three Degrees has been printed and reached a second edition in 1908. It is called the Dharma working of Craft Masonry. The variations from our own form are at once numerous and slight, but novelties are also introduced, a few of which may be tabulated: The rubrics are much fuller and make for clearness in working. The Entered Apprentice is taken three times round the Lodge and is brought back on each occasion to the center. The second circumambulations are opposite to the first, or against the sun, the third being the same as the first — otherwise following the sun. In the Second Degree, after the circumambulations, the Candidate is placed in the center and passes through five stages or experiences, corresponding to work on the Rough Stone, the Arts, the Sciences, the Humanities, and apparently rest after work, with the idea of work to follow. In the Third Degree the Obligation is shortened, more especially in respect of certain covenants on the virtue of chastity, while some of the wording differs in other clauses. The language differs throughout in many places of the Rituals and some of the prayers are changed. All essential points, however, remain — it being understood that — subject to these variations — the text follows the Scottish working. Recent rumors, however, speak of drastic changes.

ANCIENT MASONRY

In the year 1908 there was some kind of feud in London, which resulted in the foundation of an independent Society under the denomination of Ancient Masonry, one reason being that the Co-Masonry of Annie Besant involved an irresponsible headship, in opposition to Masonic principles. The new foundation abandoned Dharma workings and had recourse to those in use by the Emulation Lodge of Instruction. It works only the Three Craft Degrees, its Candidates being initiated, passed, and raised — whether male or female — precisely as those who enter Masonry under the obedience of the Grand Lodge of England. The Rev. Dr. W. F. Cobb, Rector of St. Ethelburga's, in the City of London, who had been made a Mason under the obedience of Grand Lodge but was no longer attached, became the prime mover in this work of reformation and was presumably at the head of the concern. The present Grand Mistress — who is, however, termed Grand Master, following Mrs. Besant's classification — is Mrs. Halsey, a kinswoman of the Rt. Hon. T. F. Halsey, Deputy Grand Master of England. Dr. Cobb has retired. The members, both male and female, are said to be enthusiasts, who maintain the character and spirit of the several Lodges at an exceedingly high grade, and the Ritual working is regarded as excellent. There was a time when Master Masons, not excepting Grand Officers, attended Meetings somewhat freely and are reported to have been much impressed, but an edict went forth from *Grand Lodge* in the usual belated fashion and has put a stop to this practice — at least, in part. The so-called *Ancient Masonry* is a small body in comparison with *Universal Co-Masonry*, but there is no question that, from everything ascertainable respecting modes of reception, its members — men and women — are to all intents and purposes as much Masons as if they had been admitted to membership in Freemasons' Hall itself — the question of recognition and this only excepted. As regards *La Maconnerie Mixte*, I have failed to obtain information about its welfare during the years of the Great War, except indeed that la Grande Maitresse, Mme. Maria Georges Martin, passed away on November 4, 1915, Dr. Martin himself following her on October 1, 1916.

DIFFUSION

The following particulars are drawn from a Directory of Lodges and Chapters under the Obedience of Annie Besant. Human Duty, No. 6, London. H. P. B. Lodge, No. 14, Bradford. Christian Rosenkreuz, No. 18, Edinburgh. Hermes, No. 20, London. Golden Rule, No. 21, London. Manchester Lodge, No. 22, Manchester. Emulation Lodge, No. 24, London. Harmony Lodge, No. 25, Southampton. Plato Lodge, No. 31, Leeds. Unity Lodge, No. 35, Bournemouth. Verity Lodge, No. 38, Brighton. Fidelity Lodge, No. 49, Bath. Arbor Vitae Lodge, No. 50, Letchworth. Dharma Lodge, No. 101, Benares. Sangha Lodge, No. 102, Bombay. Shanti Lodge, No. 105, Bombay. Rising Sun of India, No. 107, Adyar. Bodhi Lodge, No. 108, East Rangoon. San Francisco Lodge, No. 358, California. Helios Lodge, No. 360, Los Angeles. Unity Lodge, No. 359, Oakland, Cal. Melbourne Lodge, No. 401, Melbourne. Victorian Lodge, No. 403, Melbourne. Sydney Lodge, No. 404, Sydney, N.S.W. Brisbane Lodge, No. 405, Brisbane. Adelaide Lodge, No. 406, Adelaide. I presume that the Lodge numbers are those of the Original Roll belonging to the French Obedience and the enormous gaps between represent in this case the issue of intervening charters which are not under Theosophical influence. It will be seen that *La Maconnerie Mixte*, its derivations and developments are a power to be reckoned with and that the conventional titular description of "Clandestine Masonry" would be imbecile in reference thereto, or indeed to "Ancient" Masonry. I have seen also reports of an Amity Lodge, No. 220, Durban, South Africa, of a Star in the East Chapter of the Royal Arch, without number of location, of a Rose Croix Chapter, Tolerance, No. 2, London, and another at Edinburgh, being St. Ann, No. 3. I do not know whether the other Lodges enumerated about are confined to Craft work.

Co-Masonry

It is said that in or about 1879 several Chapters under the obedience of the Supreme Council of France, Ancient and Accepted Scottish Rite, revolted from that authority, the tendency to disturbance being as usual fomented by the Grand Orient. Whether this Obedience approved what followed I have no means of knowing, but the Chapters in question reincorporated themselves under the title of *La Grande Loge Symbolique de France*, according to the particulars before me. This statement does not appear to mean that they passed under the authority of *La Grande Loge de France*. It is impossible, however, from the confused evidence to determine this point certainly or to decide what Degrees were conferred by the new body, but they were presumably those of *Le Rit Francais* and not of the Scottish Rite. The central jurisdiction appears to have governed Lodges and not Chapters. One of the separated Lodges — the nature of whose dissatisfaction is shown by its title of *Les Libres Penseurs* — held its meetings at Pecq, a village in the Department of Seine et Oise. On November 25, 1881, this Lodge resolved that Mlle. Maria Desraimes, a writer on humanitarian subjects and the rights of women, should be admitted into Freemasonry. The proposers were M. Hubron, the WM, and six other Master Masons. The initiation took place on January 14, 1882, in the presence of Brethren drawn from all parts. From her subsequent history Mlle. Desraimes must have been also passed and raised, but there are no particulars in the sources to which I have had access. The Lodge was suspended, but whether by the Authority which it had helped to create or by some other Grand Obedience does not appear.

La Maconnerie Mixte

More than ten years passed away, during which I am unable to give any account of the lady's Masonic history. It seems certain that there was no Lodge in which she could have held Office and much less have passed the Chair. This notwithstanding she was approached in the early part of 1893 by Dr. Georges Martin, a Mason holding the Thirty-Third Degree of the A and ASR and described by himself as *feministe en meme temps que macon*. He had championed the rights of women on many occasions and in particular, being a physician himself, their capacity for admission to the medical profession. At the period in question, he was coming forward once more on the same mission, but this time asserting their title to be made Masons. With this object he resolved on establishing *La Maconnerie Mixte* and hence had recourse for assistance to the only Woman- Mason within his knowledge. The result was that on March 4, April 1 and April 4, 1893, Mlle. Desraimes, acting under his influence and presumably with his cooperation, successively initiated, passed and raised sixteen female Candidates, otherwise — in his view — a sufficient number for the constitution of a Lodge of Women. It appears to have been founded accordingly, whereupon Dr. Georges Martin demanded and acquired affiliation, in which manner the new foundation became literally a "mixed" Lodge, the location of which was Paris. A Constitution was framed under the title of *Grande Lodge Symbolique Ecossaise Mixte de France*, borrowed evidently in the main part from the schismatic body mentioned previously. It's one Lodge at the moment was called *Le Droit Humain*, and its original activities appear to have been restricted within the limits of Blue Masonry. But in 1900, the Thirty Degrees of the Ancient and Accepted Scottish Rite were superposed on those of the Craft by Dr. Georges Martin in conjunction with other Inspectors-General. A Supreme Council was established to govern the Order, to preserve the Constitution and to issue Charters, Warrants and Certificates. The titular head, Maria Desraimes, died ten months after the foundation of the First Lodge and was succeeded by Maria Georges Martin as President and RW Mistress, or Venerable. In

1901 she appears to have become Grand Mistress of the Order and President of the Supreme Council.

La Maconnnerie Mixte proved a successful experiment, and at the end of 1912 it is on record that there were 12,000 members in all parts of the world, including one hundred Lodges in the United States. England, India, Africa, Holland, South American, Oceania were embraced by its map. As regards Masonic status in France, at the date in question, no recognition of its activities was extended by the Grand Orient and affiliation to Mixed Lodges was forbidden. On the other hand, the Grande Loge de France received men who had been initiated in Mixed Lodges by a process termed regularization, while the Supreme Council went further, permitting its members to affiliate and receiving joining members from the Mixed Lodges, so only that they were males. It might apparently have exceeded this limit by establishing official relations and receiving Sisters, but it was hindered for the time being owing to "international treaties." Such is the commentary of Latin Freemasonry on the knavish assertion that it is impossible for any woman to be made a Mason.

The Life of the Mystic

There Are certain conventional terms which, on the one hand, do not accurately represent the construction placed upon them along a given line, but that construction has been accepted so long and so generally that the defect in the application may be regarded as partially effaced; and, on the other hand, there are also conventional terms between which a distinction has come into existence, although it is not justified by their primary significance. As regards the first class, the very general use of the term "occult movement" may be taken as an example. It is inexact after two manners: in involves at once too much and too little-too much, because it has served to represent a good deal that is not at all of the occult order; and too little, because a slight change in the point of view would bring within the range of its meaning many things which nobody who now uses it would think of including therein.

The doings of more than one great secret political organization might, in the full sense of the words, require to be classed as part of the occult movement, though no one will need to be informed that the latter is not political; while certain events which have occurred and are occurring in the open day, and have all along challenged the verdict of public opinion, cannot strictly be included in occultism, as they betray none of its external characteristics. I refer to the phenomena of animal magnetism, hypnotism, spiritualism, and all that which is included in the field of psychical research. In respect of the second class, a very clear differentiation now exists between the terms "occult" and "mystic," and it is one also which it is necessary to recognize, though, fundamentally speaking, the two words are identical, differing only in the fact that one of them is of Latin and the other of Greek origin By the occultist we have come to understand the disciple of one or all of the secret sciences; the student, that is to say, of alchemy, astrology, the forms and methods of divination, and of the mysteries which used to be included under the generic description of magic.

The mystic is, at the first attempt, perhaps more difficult to describe, except in the terminology of some particular school of thought; he has no concern as such with the study of the secret sciences; he does not work on materials or investigate forces which exist outside himself; but he endeavors, by a certain training and the application of a defined rule of life to reestablish correspondence with the divine nature from which, in his belief, he originated, and to which his return is only a question of time, or what is commonly understood as evolution. The distinction between the occultist and the mystic, however much the representative of physical science at the present day might be disposed to resent the imputation, is therefore, loosely speaking, and at least from one point of view, the distinction between the man of science and the man of introspection. The statement, as we shall see, is not exhaustive, and it is not indeed descriptive.

It may be said more fully, in the words of the late Edward Maitland, that the occultist is concerned with "transcendental physics, and is of the intellectual, belonging to science," while the mystic "deals with transcendental metaphysics, and is of the spiritual, belonging to religion." Expressed in modern terms, this is really the doctrine of Plotinus, which recognizes "the subsistence of another intellect, different from those which reasons, and which is denominated rational." Thus, on the one hand, there are the phenomena of the transcendental produced on the external plane, capable of verification and analysis, up to a certain point; and, on the other, there is the transcendental life. "That which is without corresponds with that which is within," says the most famous Hermetic maxim; indeed, the connection suggested is almost that of the circumference with the center; and if there is a secret of the soul expressed by the term mysticism, the phenomena of the soul manifesting on the external plane must be regarded as important; but these are the domain of occultism. The importance must, of course, differ as the phenomena fall into higher and lower; the divinations of geomancy carry an appearance of triviality, while the design of ceremonial magic to establish communication with higher orders of extra-mundane intelligence wears a momentous aspect; but both are the exercise of seership, and this gift, as a testimony of the soul and her powers, is never trivial.

Assuming therefore a relationship subsisting between occult practice and the transcendental life of the soul, it seems worthwhile to contrast for a moment the work of the mystic with that of the disciple of occult science, so as to realize as accurately as possible the points of correspondence and distinction between Ruysbroeck, St. John of the Cross and Saint-Martin, as types of the mystic school, and Arnoldus de Villanova and Martines de Pasqually, as representing the school of occult science. The examples of such a contrast must naturally be sought in the past, because, although occult science is pursued in the present day, and by some ardently, it can scarcely be said to have votaries like those who were of old. The inquiry belongs also to the past in respect of the mystic, for, to speak plainly, the saint belongs to the past. So far as the life of the outside world is concerned, there is little opportunity amidst mundane distractions for the whole-hearted labors of the other centuries. The desire for the house is indeed among us, but the zeal of it is scarcely here, not, at least, in the sense of the past.

The distinction in question is more than that which is made between the man of action and the man of reflection; it is not that which we have come to regard as differentiating the man of science from the philosopher. There are many instances of synthetic occult philosophers — among them Cornelius Agrippa and Robert Fludd — who neither divined nor evoked — who were not alchemists, astrologers, or theurgists — but rather interpreters and harmonizers; and yet these men were not mystics in the proper sense of the term. Nor is the distinction quite that which constitutes the essential difference between the saint and the specialist, though the occult student of the past was in most cases a specialist who was faithful to his branch. The activity and the strenuousness of the life was often greater with the mystic than in the case of the man who was dedicated to some division of occult knowledge, though alchemist and astrologer were both laborious men — men whose patience imbued them with something of the spirit which governs modern scientific research. The ground of the contrast is in the purpose which actuated the two schools of experience. The crucible in which metals are transmuted, on the assumption of alchemy, is still a crucible and the converted metal is still a metal; so also, the astrologer may trace the occult and imponderable influences of the stars, but the stars are material bodies.

The practical work of the mystic concerned, on the contrary, the soul's union with God, for, to state it briefly, this, and this only, is the end of mysticism. It is no study of psychic forces, nor, except incidentally, is it the story of the soul and her development, such as would be involved in the doctrine of reincarnation. It is essentially a religious experiment and is the one ultimate and real experiment designed by true religion. It is for this reason that in citing examples of mystics, I have chosen two men who were eminent for sanctity in the annals of the Christian Church, for we are concerned only with the West;

while the third, though technically out of sympathy, essentially belonged to the Church. I must not, therefore, shrink from saying that the alternative name of the mystic is that of the saint when he has attained the end of his experiment. There are also other terms by which we may describe the occultist, but they refer to the science which he followed.

The life of the mystic was then in a peculiar sense the life of sanctity. It was not, of course, his exclusive vocation; if we are to accept the occult sciences at their own valuation, more than one of them exacted, and that not merely by implication, something more than the God-fearing, clean-living spirit, which is so desirable even in the ordinary businessman. He who was in search of transmutation was counselled, in the first instance, to convert himself, and the device on the wall of his laboratory was Labora but also Ora. The astrologer, who calculated the influences of the stars on man, was taught that, in the last resource, there was a law of grace by which the stars were ruled. Even the conventional magician, he who called and controlled spirits, knew that the first condition of success in his curious art was to be superior to the weakness of the inconstant creatures whose dwelling is amidst the flux of the elements.

I have said that, in most cases, the occult student was, after his manner, a specialist — he was devoted to his particular branch. Deep down in the heart of the alchemist there may have been frequently the belief that certain times and seasons were more favorable than others for his work, and that the concealed materials which he thought of symbolically as the Sun and Moon, as Mercury, Venus or Mars, were not wholly independent of star and planet in the sky; and hence no doubt he knew enough of elementary astrology to avoid afflicted aspects and malign influences. But, outside this, the alchemist was not an astrologer, and to be wise in the lore of the stars was an ambition that was sufficient for one life, without meddling in the experiments of alchemy. On the other hand, the mystic, in common with all the members of his community, having only one object in view, and one method of pursuing it—by the inward way of contemplation—had nothing to differentiate and could not therefore specialize.

Again, occult science justifies itself as the transmission of a secret knowledge from the past, and the books which represent the several branches of this knowledge bear upon them the outward marks that they are among the modes of this transmission, without which it is certain that there would be no secret sciences. The occult student was, therefore, an initiate in the conventional sense of the term — he was taught, even in astrology. There were schools of Kabalism, schools of alchemy, schools of magic, in which the mystery of certain knowledge was imparted from adept to neophyte, from master to pupil. It is over this question of corporate union that we have at once an analogy and a distinction between the mystic and the occultist. The former, as we find him in the West, may in a sense be called an initiate because he was trained in the rule of the Church; but the historical traces of secret association for mystic objects during the Christian centuries are very slight, whereas the traces of occult association are exceedingly strong.

The mysteries of pre-Christian times were no doubt schools of mystic experience. Plato and Plotinus were assuredly mystics who were initiated in these schools. Unfortunately, the nature of this experience has come down to us, for the most part, in a fragmentary and veiled manner. But, outside exoteric writings, it has in my belief come down, and it is possible to reconstruct it, at least intellectually and speculatively, for it is embedded in the symbolic modes of advancement practiced by certain secret societies which now exist among us.

The Life of the Mystic

A transmission of mystic knowledge has therefore taken place from the past, but the evidence is of an exceedingly complex nature and cannot be explained here. Nor is it necessary to our purpose, for western mysticism is almost exclusively the gift of the Church to the West, and the experiment of Christian mysticism, without any veils or evasions, is written at large in the literature of the Church. It may call to be re-expressed for our present requirements in less restricted language, but there is not really any need to go further. "The Ascent of Mount Carmel," "The Adornment of the Spiritual Marriage," and "The Castle of the Inward Man," contain the root-matter of the whole process. I have also found it well and exhaustively described in obscure little French books which might appear at first sight to be simply devotional manuals for the use of schools and seminaries. I have found it in books equally obscure which a few decades ago would have been termed Protestant. There is the same independent unanimity of experience and purpose through all which the alchemists have claimed for their own literature, and I have no personal doubt that the true mystics of all times and countries constitute an unincorporated fellowship communicating continually together in the higher consciousness. They do not differ essentially in the East or the West, in Plotintis or in Gratry.

In its elementary presentation, the life of the mystic consists primarily in the detachment of the will from its normal condition of immersion in material things and in its redirection towards the goodwill which abides at the center. This center, according to the mystics, is everywhere and is hence, in a certain sense, to be found in all; but it is sought most readily, by contemplation, as at the center of the man himself, and this is the quest and finding of the soul. If there is not an open door — an entrance to the closed palace — within us, we are never likely to find it without us. The rest of the experiences are those of the life of sanctity leading to such a ground of divine union as is possible for humanity in this life.

In the distinction — analogical, as already said — which I have here sought to establish, there lies the true way to study the lives of the mystics and of those who graduated in the schools of occult science. The object of that study, and of all commentary arising out of such lives, is to lead those, and there are thousands, who are so constituted as to desire the light of mysticism, to an intellectual realization of that light.

The life of the mystic belongs to the divine degree, and it would be difficult to say that it is attainable in the life of the world; but some of its joys and consolations — as indeed its trials and searching — are not outside our daily ways. Apart from all the heroisms, and in the outer courts only of the greater ecstasies, there are many who would set their face towards Jerusalem if their feet were put upon the way — and would thus turn home again.

THE WORD

LANGUAGE is the outer vesture or symbol of thought within: I conceive that this is a commonplace, though it is not after all very usual and practical realization. It has been said also that words hide thought, and they do so after two manners: when there is a design of concealment in order to confuse issues, but this occasional characteristic of minds is without philosophical importance or indeed interest; when — all our effort notwithstanding — thought passes into expression with difficulty, owing to abstruse subject-matter and not to want of clearness — which again is of no interest or importance for our Masonic purpose. At its best language is in a working sacramental analogy with the concepts of mind and communicates from mind to mind within those measures. When we hear of an Incommunicable Word, we know that "word nonsense" is being talked, for that which exceeds communication also exceeds expression. If therefore the illuminated Councillor von Eckartshausen undertook a considerable journey to impart the Incommunicable Word to Baron von Liebistorf, both persons being serious, we know that the subject of communication was not a word at all and that the term incommunicable was used by way of subterfuge. So also, when we hear of a Lost Word in Masonry and collateral Rites, it is necessary to pause and consider. In the traditional history of the Third Degree that Word which passes into concealment is not by the hypothesis a thing of mystery, grace or power, but a conventional secret reserved to a certain rank. As such, it was of similar value to our old friend *ABRACADABRA*. But when, as Masters, we testify through all the years of our Masonic life that we are following the quest of this Word it assumes of necessity another aspect: it is no longer a conventional secret denoting a given status, no longer a literal word — unless indeed we are content, like De Quincey to believe that Emblematic Freemasonry is the great imposture of the modern world. This being so, what is the position of those Degrees — very high and important in Masonry — which exist for the purpose of communicating the Lost Word in the form of a verbal convention? They appear stultified by the very fact: such, however, is not the case. The Degrees in question are simply remaining as they must within the measures of Masonic sacrament and symbol. While it is essential, to justify Masonry, that its quest must end in attainment, it can end only as it began, namely, as a system veiled in allegory and illustrated by symbols. But we have a right to expect that the meaning behind the allegory and the grace behind the symbols should be of such kind that we are not unwarranted in having followed the long quest through many Rites and Grades. No, albeit on account of certain covenants I am limited to a simple affirmative, I place on record here, as one who has followed the quest and has reached its term in symbolism, that it is amply warranted by that infinite realm of grace and truth in God which opens out, for those who can discern it, beyond the scheme of the Grades as displayed in their Ritual procedure. I speak of the Third Degree, the Holy Royal Arch and certain Christian Orders in Masonry.

WORD AND LIFE

It follows that when the lost Arcanum is restored — within or without Masonry — it can only pass into expression as a word or words which will convey nothing to the uninitiated, nor does the bare fact of its communications within the Mysteries of a particular Fraternity signify anything of vital import to a member not otherwise prepared for the reception of real knowledge. The outer form is, so to speak, the vehicle or body of the grace, independently of which the latter cannot be conveyed, any more than the soul of a human being can function in the material world apart from a physical body as the means of communicating with that world. It may be that this is only an elaborate way of affirming that all the great things of life are outside evidence and that their appeal — in the last resource — is scarcely to the logical understanding, though I incline to think that something of the best and highest is reflected therein and is also represented thereby after its own manner. That Word, with the mystery of which I am dealing only so far as it is expressed in Masonic symbolism, is imparted — as we have seen — to the adept at one or another epoch of his advancement; but its meaning is not imparted, except by secret communication between his own soul and the truth which is behind the symbol. Explicitly or implicitly, it always stands for a Word of Life. It may act on those who can receive it as an awakening of the soul's consciousness in the direction of things that are Divine and the first participation of human in Divine Nature. Here is the sense in which man is saved by the power of the Name *Yeheshuah*; this is the abiding presence signified by that of *Immanuel*, the grace from everlasting to everlasting in the mystic cipher *I.N.R.I.*, and the eternal mercy which is *Jehovah*. But in the Lodges of Mount Sinai and the Chapters of Holy Sanctuary the Words and Names are recited as things spoken with the lips and received into physical ears: except to the very few they do not stand for life. There is no translation of symbols so that allegories testify full of meaning from within and that pageants move not only in ordered sequence but in the grace of God and His power. It comes about therefore that the Word is lost even in its recovery. Peace has departed from the Tabernacles and light out of the Holy Places, the Sacred Cities remain unfinished, and the Sanctuary can be erected only in the heart of the elect because the Word of Life is lost.

WORD IN KABALISM

The Most Holy and Eternal Logos of the Fourth Gospel has its analogue in Kabalism, and indeed the intimations thereon of this Secret Tradition in later Israel are very often of the nature of root-identity rather than of simple correspondence. Because there is a quest pursued in Masonry, which is concerned with the loss and recovery of a Word, it is desirable to indicate briefly that there are other and not less pregnant aspects of the subject than have been dealt with already in my consideration of the Sacred Name Jehovah. According to the *Zohar*, when Scripture says that the Lord shewed Himself to Abraham in the plains of Mamre, that which manifested was the Word. The reference is to Genesis XVIII I. I believe that there are certain side-issues of Christian theology, according to which He Who is the Word appears as the self-revealing mode of Deity, in what I may call the personal manifestations of the Divine throughout the Old Testament. He it was therefore — on this understanding — Who walked with Adam in the cool of the evening, Who appeared to Moses in the burning bush, Who delivered the Law on Mount Sinai, Who spoke in the darkness to Samuel. In consonance herewith the momentous paraphrase of Onkelos substitutes Memrah = Word in place of Jehovah. So also the Targum of Jonathan translates Bereshith — the first word in Genesis — as Wisdom, which is wholly in consonance with the Secret Tradition, and Wisdom in this case is a synonym of the Word, considered as the Divine Seed which — according to the *Zohar* — brought forth the whole creation: "in the beginning" — which is the Wisdom of the Word — "God created the heaven and the earth."

THE TEMPLAR ORDERS IN FREEMASONRY
*An Historical Consideration of their
Origin and Development*

HAVING REGARD the fact that Emblematic Freemasonry, as it is known and practiced at this day, arose from an Operative Guild and within the bosom of a development from certain London Lodges which prior to the year 1717 had their titles in the past of the Guild and recognized its Old Charges, it would seem outside the reasonable likelihood of things that less than forty years after the foundation of Grand Lodge Knightly Orders should begin to be heard of developing under the aegis of the Craft, their titles in some cases being borrowed from the old institutions of Christian Chivalry. It is this, however, which occurred, and the inventions were so successful that they multiplied on every side, from 1754 to the threshold of the French Revolution, new denominations being devised when the old titles were exhausted. There arose in this manner a great tree of Ritual, and it happens, moreover, that we are able to affirm the kind of root from which it sprang. Twenty years after the date of the London Grand Lodge, and when that of Scotland may not have been twelve months old, the memorable Scottish Freemason, Andrew Michael Ramsay, delivered an historical address in a French Lodge, in the course of which he explained that the Masonic Brotherhood arose in Palestine during the period of the Crusades, under the protection of Christian Knights, with the object of restoring Christian Churches which had been destroyed by Saracens in the Holy Land.

For some reason which does not emerge, the foster-mother of Masonry, according to the mind of the hypothesis, was the Chivalry of St. John. Ramsay appears to have left the

Masonic arena, and he died in the early part of 1743, but his discourse produced a profound impression on French Freemasonry. He offered no evidence, but France undertook to produce it after its own manner and conformably to the spirit of the time by the creation of Rites and Degrees of Masonic Knighthood, no trace of which is to be found prior to Ramsay. Their prototypes of course were extant, the Knights of Malta, Knights of the Holy Sepulchre, Knights of St. Lazarus, in the gift of the Papal See, and the Order of Christ in Portugal, in the gift of the Portuguese Crown. There is no need to say that these Religious and Military Orders have nothing in common with the Operative Masonry of the past, and when their titles were borrowed for the institution of Masonic Chivalries, it is curious how little the latter owed to the ceremonial of their precursors, in their manners of making and installing Knights, except in so far as the general prototype of all is found in the Roman Pontifical. There are, of course, reflections and analogies: in the old knightly corporations the candidate was required to produce proofs of noble birth, and the Strict Observance demanded these at the beginning, but owing to obvious difficulties is said to have ended by furnishing patents at need; in the Military Order of Hospitallers of the Holy Sepulchre of Jerusalem, he undertook, as in others, to protect the Church of God, with which may be compared modern Masonic injunctions in the Temple and Holy Sepulchre to maintain and defend the Holy Christian Faith; again at his Knighting he was "made, created and constituted now and forever," which is identical, word for word, with the formula of another Masonic Chivalry, and will not be unknown to many.

But the appeal of the new foundations was set in another direction and was either to show that they derived from Masonry or were Masonry itself at the highest, in the proper understanding thereof. When the story of a secret perpetuation of the old Knights Templar — outside the Order of Christ —

arose in France or Germany, but as I tend to conclude in France, it was and remains the most notable case in point of this appeal and claim. It rose up within Masonry, and it came about that the Templar element overshadowed the dreams and pretensions of other Masonic Chivalries, or, more correctly, outshone them all. I am dealing here with matters of fact and not proposing to account for the facts themselves within the limits of a single study. The Chevalier Ramsay never spoke of the Templars: his affirmation was that the hypothetical building confraternity of Palestine united ultimately with the Knights of St. John of Jerusalem; that it became established in various countries of Europe as the Crusaders drifted back; and that its chief center in the thirteenth century was Kilwinning in Scotland. But the French or otherwise German Masonic mind went to work upon this thesis, and in presenting the Craft with the credentials of Knightly connections it substituted the Order of the Temple for the chivalry chosen by Ramsay. The Battle of Lepanto and the Siege of Vienna had invested the annals of the St. John Knighthood with a great light of valor; but this was as little and next to nothing in comparison with the talismanic attraction which for some reason attached to the Templar name and was obviously thrice magnified when the proposition arose that the great chivalry had continued to exist in secret from the days of Philippe le Bel even to the second half of the eighteenth century. There were other considerations, however, which loomed largely, and especially regarding the sudden proscription which befell the Order in 1307. Of the trial which followed there were records available to all, in successive editions of the French work of Dupuy, first published in 1685; in the German Historical Tractatus of Petrus Puteamus published at Frankfort in 1665; in Gurther's Latin Historia Tempiarsorum of 1691; and in yet other publications prior to 1750. There is not a little evidence of one impression which was produced by these memorials, the notion, namely, of an unexplored realm of mystery extending behind the charges. It was the day of Voltaire, and it happened that a shallow infidelity was characterized by the kind of license which fosters intellectual extravagance, by a leaning in directions which are generally termed superstitious — though superstition itself was pilloried — and by attraction towards occult arts and supposed hidden knowledge. Advanced persons were ceasing to believe in the priest but were disposed to believe in the sorcerer, and the Templars had been accused of magic, of worshipping a strange idol, the last suggestion — for some obscure reason — being not altogether indifferent to many who had slipped the anchor of their faith in God. Beyond these frivolities and the foolish minds that cherished them, there were other persons who were neither in the school of a rather cheap infidelity nor in that of common superstition, but who looked seriously for light to the East and for its imagined traditional wisdom handed down from past ages. They may have been dreamers also, but they were less or more zealous students after their own manner; within their proper measures, and the Templar Chivalry drew them because they deemed it not unlikely that its condemnation by the paramount orthodoxy connoted a suspicion that the old Knighthood had learned in Palestine more than the West could teach. Out of such elements were begotten some at least of the Templar Rites and they grew from more to more, till this particular aspect culminated in the Templar dramas of Werner, in which an Order concealed through the ages and perpetuated through saintly custodians reveals to a chosen few among Knights Templar some part of its secret doctrine — the identity of Christ and Horus, of Mary the Mother of God, and Isis the Queen of Heaven. The root of these dreams on doctrine and myth transfigured through the ages — with a heart of reality behind it — will be found, as it seems to me, in occult derivations from Templar Ritual which belong to circa 1782 and are still in vigilant custody on the continent of Europe. I mention this lest it should be thought that the intimations of a German poet, though he was an active member of the Strict Observance, were mere inventions of an imaginative mind.

There is no historical evidence for the existence of any Templar perpetuation story prior to the Oration of Ramsay, just as there is no question that all documents produced by the French non-Masonic Order of the Temple, founded in the early years of the nineteenth century, are inventions of that period and are fraudulent like the rest of its claim, its list of Grand Masters included. There is further — as we have observed — no evidence of any Rite or Degree of Masonic Chivalry prior to 1737, to which date is referred the discourse of Ramsay. That this was the original impetus which led to their production may be regarded as beyond dispute, and it was the case especially with Masonic Templar revivals. Their thesis was his thesis varied. For example, according to the Rite of the Strict Observance the proscribed Order was carried by its Marshal, Pierre d'Aumont, who escaped with a few other Knights to the Isles of Scotland, disguised as Operative Masons. They remained there and under the same veil the Templars continued to exist in secret from generation to generation under the shadow of the mythical Mount Heredom of Kilwinning. To whatever date the old dreams ascribe it, when Emblematic Freemasonry emerged it was — *ex hypothesi* — a product of the union between Knights Templar and ancient Scottish Masonry. Such is the story told.

The Strict Observance was founded by Baron von Hund in Germany between about 1751 and 1754 to 1755 and is usually regarded as the first Masonic Chivalry which put forward the story of Templar perpetuation. I have accepted this view on my own part, but subject to his claim at its value — if any — that he had been made a Knight of the Temple in France, some twelve years previously. The question arises, therefore, as to the fact or possibility of antecedent Degrees of the kind in that country, and we are confronted at once by many stories afloat concerning the Chapter of Clermont, the foundation of which at Paris is referred to several dates. It was in existence, according to Yarker, at some undetermined period before 1742, for at that date its Masonic Rite, consisting of three Degrees superposed on those of the Craft, was taken to Hamburg. A certain Von Marshall, whose name belongs to the history of the Strict Observance, had been admitted in the previous year, Von Hund himself following in 1743 — not at Hamburg, but at Paris — for all of which no authority is cited and imagination may seem to have been at work. But some of the statements, including those of other English writers, are ascribable to a source in Thory's *Acta Latamorum*. When Woodford speaks of Von Hund's admission into Templar Masonry at Clermont as not a matter of hypothesis, but of certain knowledge, he is dependent on the French historian, according to whom the German Baron was made a Mason at Paris in 1742. The Chapter of Clermont was founded in that city as late as 1754, with the result that he derived Templar teaching from Clermont, on which he built up the Observance system. But whatever the point is worth, this story is not only at issue with that of Von Hund himself, but with the current chronology of the Observance. To involve matters further, the Chapter is reported otherwise to have derived its Templar element from something unspecified at Lyons which is referred to 1738. The utmost variety of statements will be found, moreover, as to the content of the Clermont Rite, the Templar character of which has also been challenged. It is proposed otherwise that the Chapter was founded on a scale of considerable magnitude, that it was installed in a vast building, and that it attracted the higher classes of French Freemasons, which notwithstanding it ceased to exist in 1758, being absorbed by the Council of Emperors established in that year for the promulgation of a different Grade system.

The Templar Orders in Freemasonry

I am in a position to reflect some light for the relief of these complications by reference to Dutch archives which have come to my knowledge. The date of the Chapter's foundation remains uncertain, but it was in activity between 1756 and 1763, so that it was not taken over — as Gould suggests — by those Masonic Emperors to whom we are indebted for the first form of the Scottish Rite, Ancient and Accepted. It is not impossible that its foundation is ascribable to the first of these dates, when it superposed on the three Craft Grades as follows: Grade of Scottish Master of St. Andrew of the Thistle, being the Fourth Grade of Masonry, "in which allegory dissolves"; Grade of Sublime Knight of God and of his Temple, being the Fifth and Last Grade of Free Masonry. At a later period, however, it became the Seventh Grade of the Rite, owing to the introduction of an Elect Degree which took the number 5 under the title of Knight of the Eagle, followed by an Illustrious Degree, occupying the sixth place and denominated Knight of the Holy Sepulchre. The Grade final in both enumerations — otherwise Knight of God — presented a peculiar, as it was also an early version of the perpetuation story, from which it follows that the Clermont Rite was Templar.

I have so far failed to trace any copy of the Ritual in this country except for that which has been placed recently in my hands, an example of the discoveries that await research in continental archives. The Templar element — which may be called the historical part is combined with a part of symbolism — for though allegory is said to be abandoned in the Fourth Degree, its spiritual sister is always present in Ritual. The aspect which it assumes in the present case is otherwise known in Masonry, the Chapter representing the Holy City, the New Jerusalem, with its twelve gates, as a tabernacle of God with men. The Candidate is represented therefore as seeking the light of glory and a perfect recompense, while that which he is promised is an end to toils and trials. He is obligated as at the gates of the city and is promised the Grand Secret of those who abide therein. The city is — spiritually speaking — in the world to come, and the reward of chivalry is there; but there is a reward also on earth within the bonds of the Order, because this is said to be divine and possessed of the treasures of wisdom. The kind of wisdom and the nature of the Great Secret is revealed in the Perpetuation Story, and so far as I am aware offers the only instance of such a claim being made on behalf of the Templars, in or out of Masonry. It belongs to a subject which engrossed the zeal of thousands throughout the seventeenth century and had many disciples — indeed, there were thousands also — during the Masonic Age which followed. The story is that the Templars began in poverty, but Baldwin II, King of Jerusalem, gave them a house in the vicinity of the site where Solomon's Temple was built of old. When it was put in repair by Hugh de Payens and the rest of the first Brethren, their digging operations unearthed an iron casket which contained priceless treasures, and chief among all the true process of the Great Work in Alchemy, the secret of transmuting metals, as communicated to Solomon by the Master Hiram Abiff. So and so only was it possible to account for the wealth of adornment which characterized the First Temple. The discovery also explains the wealth acquired by the Templars, but it led in the end to their destruction. Traitors who knew of the secret, though they had not themselves attained it, revealed the fact to Clement V and Philip the Fair of France, and the real purpose of the persecution which followed was to wrest the transmuting process from the hands of its custodians. Jacques de Molay and his co-heirs died to preserve it, but three of the initiated Knights made their escape and after long wandering from country to country they found refuge in the caves of Mount Heredom. They were succored by Knights of St. Andrew of the Thistle, with whom they made an alliance and on whom they conferred their knowledge. To conceal it from others and yet transmit it through the ages they created the Masonic Order in 1340; but the alchemical secret, which is the physical term of the Mystery, has been ever reserved to those who can emerge from the veils of allegory — that is to say, for the chiefs of St. Andrew of the Thistle, who are Princes of the Rosy Cross, and the Grand Council of the Chapter.

The alchemical side of this story is in a similar position to that of the perpetuation myth, of which it is an early version. There is nothing that can be taken seriously. But this is not to say that in either case there is no vestige of possibilities behind. Modern science tends more and more to show us that the transmutation of metals is not an idle dream and — speaking on my own part — there are well-known testimonies in the past on the literal point of fact which I and others have found it difficult to set utterly aside. So also, there are few things more certain in history than is the survival of Knights Templar after their proscription and suspension as an Order. With this fact in front of us it is not as a hypothesis improbable that there or here the chivalry may have been continued in secret by the making of new Knights. It is purely a question of evidence, and this is unhappily wanting. The traditional histories of Knightly Masonic Degrees — like those of the Chapter of Clermont, the Strict Observance and the Swedish Rite — bear all the marks of manufacture; the most that can be said concerning them — and then in the most tentative manner — is that by bare possibility there may have been somewhere in the world a rumor of secret survival, in which case the root matter of their stories would not have been pure invention. The antecedent material would then have been worked over and adapted to Masonic purposes, inspired by the Oration of Ramsay.

It is to be presumed that when this speculation is left to stand at its value, there is no critical mind which will dream of an authentic element in Hugh de Payen's supposed discovery of the Powder of Projection at or about the site of the Jewish

Temple. This romantic episode stands last in a series of similar fictions which are to be found in the history of Alchemy. When we are led to infer therefore by the records before me that the Chapter of Clermont reached its end circa 1763, we shall infer that it was in a position no longer to carry on the pretense of possessing and being able to communicate at will the Great Secret of Alchemy. It is evident from the Ritual that this was not disclosed to those who, being called in their turn, were admitted to the highest rank, and became Knights of God. It was certainly promised, however, at a due season as a reward of merit. From a false pretense of this kind the only way of escape would be found by falling back upon renounced and abjured allegory. Now, we have seen that the Chapter in its last Degree represented the New Jerusalem, and therefore its alchemy might well be transferred from a common work in metals to the spiritual side of Hermeticism. Those who have read Robert Fludd and Jacob Bohme will be acquainted with this aspect; but it may not have satisfied the figurative Knights of God, who had come so far in their journey from the Lodge of Entered Apprentice to a Temple of supposed adeptship. The Chapter therefore died.

  I have met with another French Ritual in a great manuscript collection and again — so far as ascertained — it seems to be the sole copy in England, though it is not unknown by name, in view of the bibliographies of Kloss and Wolfsteig. It is called Le Chevalier du Temple, and is of high importance to our subject. The collection to which I refer is in twelve volumes, written on old rag paper, the watermark of which shows royal arms and the lilies of France: it is pre-French Revolution and post 1768 say, on a venture, about 1772. The Ritual to which I refer extends from p. 73 to 202 of the fifth volume, in a size corresponding to what is termed crown octavo among us. The hand is clear and educated. The particular Templar Chivalry is represented as an Order connected with and acknowledging nothing else in Freemasonry except the Craft Degrees. In respect of antiquity, it claims descent by succession from certain Canons or Knights of the Holy Sepulchre, who first bore the Red Cross on their hearts, and were founded by James the First, brother of the first Bishop of Jerusalem. These Canons became the Knights Hospitallers of a much later date. On these followed the Templars, from whom the Masonic Knights of the Temple more especially claimed derivation, though in some obscure manner they held descent from all, possibly in virtue of spiritual consanguinity postulated between the various Christian chivalries of Palestine. The traditional history of the Grade is given at unusual length and is firstly that of the Templars, from their foundation to their sudden failure, the accusations against them included; it is a moderately accurate summary, all things considered. There is presented in the second place a peculiar version of the perpetuation story which is designed on the one hand to indicate the fact of survival in several directions, and on the other to make it clear that Templar Masonry had in view no scheme of vengeance against Popes and Kings. After the proscription of the chivalry it is affirmed that those who remained over were scattered through various countries, desolate and rejected everywhere. A few in their desperation joined for reprisals, but their conspiracy is characterized as detestable, and its memory is held in horror. It fell to pieces speedily for want of recruits. Among the other unfortunate Knights who had escaped destruction, a certain number entered also into a secret alliance and chose as time went on their suitable successors among persons of noble and gentle birth, with a view to perpetuate the Order and in the hope at some favorable epoch that they would be restored to their former glory and reenter into their possessions. We hear nothing of Kilwinning or Heredom, and indeed no one country is designated as a place of asylum; but it is affirmed that this group of survivors created Freemasonry and its three Craft

Degrees to conceal from their enemies the fact that the Chivalry was still in being and to test aspirants who entered the ranks, so that none but those who were found to be of true worth and fidelity should be advanced from the Third Degree into that which lay beyond. To such as were successful the existence of the secret chivalry became known only at the end of seven years, three of which were passed as Apprentice, two as Companion or Fellow Craft, and two as Master Mason. It was on the same conditions and with the same objects that the Order in the eighteenth century was prepared to receive Masons who had been proved into that which was denominated the Illustrious Grade and Order of Knights of the Temple of Jerusalem.

The Candidate undertakes in his Obligation to do all in his power for the glorious restoration of the Order; to succor his Brethren in their need; to visit the poor, the sick and the imprisoned; to love his King and his religion; to maintain the State; to be ever ready in his heart for all sacrifice in the cause of the faith of Christ, for the good of His Church and its faithful. The Pledge is taken on the knees, facing a tomb of black marble which represents that of Molay, the last Grand Master and martyr-in-chief of the Order. Thereafter the inward meaning of the three Craft Degrees is explained to the Candidate. That of Apprentice recalls the earliest of Christian chivalries, being the Canons or Knights of the Holy Sepulchre, who for long had no distinctive clothing and hence the divested state of the Masonic Postulant. But this state signified also that his arm is ever ready to do battle with the enemies of the Holy Christian Religion and his heart for the sacrifice of his entire being to Jesus Christ. The alleged correspondences and meanings are developed at some length, but it will be sufficient to mention that the Masonic Candidate enters the Lodge poor and penniless, because that was the condition at their beginning of the Templars and the other Orders of Christian Knighthood.

The Candidate is prepared for the Second Craft Degree in a somewhat different manner from that of the First, and this has reference to certain distinctions between the clothing of a Knight of the Holy Sepulchre and that of a Knight of St. John. The seven steps are emblematic of the seven sacraments of the Holy Church, by the help of which the Christian Chivalries maintained their faith against the infidel, and also of the seven deadly sins which they trampled under their feet. The Blazing Star inscribed with the letter Yod, being the initial letter of the Name of God in Hebrew, signified the Divine Light which enlightened the Chivalries and was ever before their eyes, as it must be also present for ever before the mind's eye of the Masonic Templars, a sacred symbol placed in the center of the building. In French Freemasonry the Pillar B belonged to the Second Degree and was marked with this letter, which had reference to Baldwin, King of Jerusalem, who provided a House for the Templars in the Holy City.

The Traditional History of the Master Grade is that of the martyrdom of Jacques de Molay, the last Grand Master of the Temple. The three assassins answered to Philip the Fair, Pope Clement V and the Prior of Montfaucon, a Templar of Toulouse, who is represented as undergoing a sentence of imprisonment for life at Paris on account of his crimes, by the authority of the Grand Master. He is said to have betrayed the Order by making false accusations and thus secured his release. The initials of certain Master Words are J.B.M., and they are also those of Jacobus Burgundus Molay.

The Chevalier du Temple has unfortunately no history, so far as I have been able to trace. I have met with it as a bare title in one other early collection, which has become known to me by means of a Dutch list of MSS., and there is no need to say that it occurs in the nomenclature of Ragon. It is numbered 69 in the archives of the Metropolitan Chapter of France, and 8 in the Rite of the Philalethes: they may or may not refer to the same Ritual as that which I have summarized here. There is no means of knowing. In any case the 36th Grade of Mizraim and the 34th of Memphis, which became No. 13 in the Antient and Primitive Rite, is to be distinguished utterly: it is called Knight of the Temple, but has no concern with the Templars and is quite worthless. It should be added that in one of the discourses belonging to Le Chevalier du Temple there is a hostile allusion to the existing multiplicity of Masonic and pseudo-Masonic Grades, and this may suggest that it is late in the order of time. A great many were, however, in evidence by and before the year 1759. We should remember Gould's opinion that there was an early and extensive propagation of Ecossais Grades, and the source of these was obviously in the Ramsay hypothesis. It is certain also that Elu Grades were not far in the rear. The date of the particular Collection Maconnique on which I depend is, of course, not that of its contents. On the whole there seems nothing to militate against a tentative or provisional hypothesis that Chevalier de Temple was no later and may have been a little earlier than the Clermont Knight of God, thus giving further color to the idea that Templar Masonry and its perpetuation story arose where it might have been expected that they would arise, in France and not in Germany. I have said that the Grade under notice has no reference to Scotland or to any specific place of Templar refuge after the proscription. But the chivalrous origin of Masonry is not less a Ramsay myth, and it characterizes almost every variant of Templar perpetuation which has arisen under a Masonic aegis, from that of the Knights of God and the Chevalier du Temple to that of Werner and his Sons of the Valley, belonging to the year 1803. There stand apart only the English Religious and Military Order and the late French Order of the Temple which depends on the Charter of Larmenius, but this was not Masonic, though its pretense of Templar perpetuation and succession is most obviously borrowed from Masonry. In conclusion, I shall think always that Baron von Hund drew from France, whether directly at Paris or via Hamburg in his own country.

We have seen that the Strict Observance appeared in Germany between 1751 and 1755, a development according to its founder of something which he had received in France so far back as 1743. No reliance can be placed on this statement, nor is the year 1751 in a much better position. Hund is supposed to have founded a Chapter of his Templar Rite about that time on his own estate at Unwurdi, where the scheme of the Order was worked out. We hear also of a later scheme, belonging to 1755 and dealing with financial matters. But the first evidential document is a Plan of the Strict Observance, laying claim on January 13, 1766, as its date of formulation, and there is a record of the Observance Master Grade, with a Catechism attached thereto, belonging to the same year. But as 1751 seems too early for anything in the definite sense 1766 is much too late. A memoir of Herr von Kleefeld by J. C. Schubert bears witness to the former's activities on behalf of the Strict Observance between 1763 and 1768. The Rite, moreover, was sufficiently important in 1763 for an impostor named Johnson to advance his claims upon it and to summon a Congress at Altenberg in May 1764, as an authorized ambassador of the Secret Headship or Sovereign Chapter in Scotland. His mission was to organize the Order in Germany, and for a time Von Hund accepted and submitted, from which it follows that his own Rite was still in very early stages. I make no doubt that it made a beginning privately circa 1755, and that a few persons were knighted, but Von Hund had enough on his hands owing to the seven years' war, so that from 1756 to 1763 there could have been little opportunity for Templar Grades under his custody, either on his own estates or elsewhere. Meanwhile the Clermont Rite was spreading in Germany and in 1763 there were fifteen Chapters in all. There is hence an element which seems nearer certitude rather than mere speculation in proposing that the Templar claim on Masonry was imported from France into Germany, that Von Hund's business was to derive and vary, not to create the thesis. Of the great success which awaited the Strict Observance, once it was fairly launched, of its bid for supremacy over all continental Masonry and of the doom which befell it because no investigation could substantiate any of its claims, there is no opportunity to speak here. It may be said that a final judgment was pronounced against it in 1782 when the Congress of Wilhelmsbad set aside the Templar claim and approved the Rectified Rite, otherwise a transformed Strict Observance, created within the bosom of the Loge de Bienfaisance at Lyons and ratified at a Congress held in that city prior to the assembly at Wilhelmsbad. The Grades of the Strict Observance superposed on the Craft were those of Scottish Master, Novice, and Knight Templar; those of the revision comprised a Regime Ecossais, described as Ancient and Rectified, and an Ordre Interieur, being Novice and Knight Beneficent of the Holy City. It laid claim on a spiritual consanguinity only in respect of the Templar Chivalry, apart from succession and historical connection, but it retained a certain root, the poetic development of which is in Werner's Sons of the Valley already mentioned, being the existence from time immemorial of a Secret Order of Wise Masters in Palestine devoted to the work of initiation for the building of a spiritual city and as such the power behind the Temple, as it was also behind Masonry.

In conclusion as to this part of my subject, the combined influence of the Templar element in the Chapter of Clermont and that of the Strict Observance which superseded it had an influence on all Continental Masonry which was not only wide and general, but lasting in the sense that some part of it has persisted there and here to the present day. The eighth Degree of the Swedish Rite, being that of Master of the Temple, communicated its particular version of the perpetuation myth, being that Molay revealed to his nephew Beaujeu, shortly before his death, the Rituals and Treasures of the Order; that the latter escaped, apparently, with these and with the disinterred ashes of the master, and was accompanied by nine other Knights, all disguised as Masons; that they found refuge among the stonemasons. It is said that in Denmark the history of Masonry, owing to the activity of a Mason named Schubert, became practically that of the Observance, until 1785, when the Rectified Rite was introduced as an outcome of the Congress of Wilhelmsbad. It was not until 1853 that the Swedish Rite replaced all others, by reason of a royal decree. As late as 1817 the Rectified Rite erected a central body in Brussels. In 1765 the Observance entered Russia and was followed by the Swedish Rite on an authorized basis in 1775. Poland and Lithuania became a diocese of the Observance Order in 1770, and it took over the Warsaw Lodges in 1773. The story of its influence in Germany itself is beyond my scope. It is written at large everywhere: at Hamburg from 1765, when Schubert founded an independent Prefectory, to 1781 (when the Rectified Rite was established for a brief period by Prince Karl von Hesse); at Nuremberg in 1765, under the same auspices; in the Grand Lodge of Saxony from circa 1762 to 1782; at Berlin, in the Mother Lodge of the Three Globes, from 1766 to 1779, when the Rosicrucians intervened; at Konigsberg from 1769 to 1799 in the Provincial Grand Lodge; in the Kingdom of Hanover, at the English Provincial Grand Lodge, from 1766 to 1778; and even now the list is not exhausted. The explanation of this influence through all its period and everywhere is that which lay behind the romantic thesis of Ramsay, as shown by his work on the Philosophical Principles of Natural and Revealed Religion, published in 1748 — I refer to the notion that there was a Mystery of Hidden Knowledge perpetuated in the East from the days of Noah and the Flood; that which lay behind, as already mentioned, the talismanic attraction exercised on Masonic minds in the eighteenth century by the name of

Knights Templar, because the Church had accused them. They had learned strange things in the East: for some it corresponded to the view of Ramsay, for others to occult knowledge on the side of Magic, and for the Chapter of Clermont to Alchemy. The collapse of the Strict Observance was not so much because it could not produce its hypothetical unknown superiors, but because it could not exhibit one shred or vestige of the desired secret knowledge.

I have now accounted at length for that which antecedes the present English Military and Religious Order of the Temple and Holy Sepulchre, so far as possible within the limits at my disposal. The Clerical Knights Templar, which originated at Weimar with the Lutheran theologian, J. A. von Starck, and presented its claims on superior and exclusive knowledge to the consideration of the Strict Observance about 1770, represent an intervention of that period which has been judged — justly or not — without any knowledge of the vast mass of material which belongs thereto and of which I had not even dreamed. The fact at least of its existence is now before me, and I await an opportunity to examine it. I can say only now that it was devised, as my reference shows, to create an impression that an alleged Spiritual Branch of the old Knights Templar possessed their real secrets and had been perpetuated to modern times. It was, therefore, in a position to supply what the Strict Observance itself wanted, but the alleged Mysteries of the Order appear to be those of Paracelsus and of Kabalism on the magical side. I have left over also: Les Chevaliers de la Palestine, otherwise Knights of Jerusalem, because although it is a Templar Grade, it is concerned with the old chivalry at an early period of its history, and not with its transmission to modern times; the Grade of Grand Inspector, otherwise Kadosh, though I am acquainted with a very early and unknown Ritual, because it does not add to our knowledge in respect of the Templar claim on Masonry. In the earliest form it shows that the judgment incurred by those who betrayed, spoliated and destroyed the Order had been imposed Divinely; that the hour of vengeance was therefore fulfilled, and that the call of Kadosh Knights was to extirpate within them those evil tendencies which would betray, spoliate and destroy the soul. Sublime Prince of the Royal Secret, because in the sources with which I am acquainted it recites the migrations of Templars and only concerns us in so far as it reproduces and varies the Ramsay thesis in respect of Masonic connections. It is important from this point of view. Sovereign Grand Inspector General, because I have failed so far to meet with any early codex, and that of Ragon is a Templar Grade indeed but concerned more especially with wreaking a ridiculous vengeance on the Knights of Malta, to whom some of the Templar possessions were assigned. Knight Commander of the Templar, because, according to the plenary ritual manuscript of Albert Pike, it is exceedingly late and is concerned in his version with the foundation and history of the Teutonic Chivalry, which is beside our purpose.

In respect of the English Military and Religious Order, I have met with nothing which gives the least color to a supposition of Gould that it arose in France: the Chevalier du Temple is its nearest analogy in that country, but the likeness resides in the fact that both Orders or Degrees have a certain memorial in the center of the Chapter or Preceptory: we know that which it represents in at least one case and in the other, as we have seen, it is the tomb of the last Grand Master. But failing an origin in France it is still less likely that it originated elsewhere on the continent, as, for example, in Germany. I conclude, therefore, that it is of British birth and growth, though so far as records are concerned it is first mentioned in America, in the Minutes of a Royal Arch Chapter, dated August 28, 1769. I have sought to go further back and so far, have failed. It was certainly working at Bristol in 1772, and two years later is heard of in Ireland. It is a matter of deep regret that I can contribute nothing to so interesting and vital a question, which appeals especially to myself on account of the beauty and spiritual significance of the Ritual in all its varied forms. The number of these may be a source of surprise to many, and I have pointed out elsewhere that however widely and strangely they differ from each other they have two points of agreement: there is no traditional history presenting a perpetuation myth or a claim on the past of chivalry, while except in one very late instance, there is no historical account whatever; and they are concerned with the one original Templar purpose, that of guarding the Holy Sepulchre and pilgrims to the Holy Places. They offer no version of Masonic origins, no explanation of Craft Symbolism, no suggestion of a secret science behind the Temple, no plan of restoring the Order to its former glory, and, above all, to its former possessions. The issue is direct and simple, much too simple and far too direct for a Continental source. Moreover, the kind of issue would have found no appeal in France; for example, or Germany, because there was no longer any need in fact to guard the tomb of Christ, and there were no pilgrims in the sense of crusading times. Finally, they would not have allegorized subjects of this kind.

I am acquainted personally with nine codices of the Ritual, outside those which belong to Irish workings, past and present, an opportunity to examine which I am hoping to find. The most important are briefly these: That of the Baldwyn Encampment at Bristol, which is probably the oldest of all: the procedure takes place while a vast army of Saracens is massing outside the Encampment. That of the Early Grand Rite of Scotland, subsequently merged in the Scottish Chapter General: The Pilgrim comes to lay the sins and follies of a lifetime at the foot of the Cross, and he passes through various symbolical veils by which the encampment is guarded. That connected with the name of Canongate Kilwinning under the title of Knight Templar Masonry, in which there is a pilgrimage to Jericho and the Jordan. That of St. George Aboyne Templar Encampment at Aberdeen, a strange elaborate pageant, in which the Candidate has a searching examination on matters of Christian doctrine. That of the Royal, Exalted, Military and Holy Order of Knights of the Temple, in the library of Grand Lodge. It represents a revision of working and belongs to the year 1830. It is of importance as a stage in the development of the English Military Order. That which Matthew Cooke presented to Albert Pike, by whom it was printed in the year 1851. It is practically the same as ours and was ratified at the Grand Conclave on April 11 of that year. That of the Religious and Military Order, of the grace and beauty of which I have no need to speak. The two that remain over are Dominion Rituals of the Order of the Temple, being that in use by the Sovereign Great Prior of Canada prior to 1876, and that which was adopted at this date under the auspices of the Grand Master, Wm. J. B. MacLeod Moore. They are of considerable interest as variants of the English original, but the second differs from all other codices by the introduction of three historical discourses, dealing with the origin of the Templar Chivalry, its destruction and its alleged Masonic connections, which are subject to critical examination, the conclusion reached being that the Templar system is Masonic only in the sense that none but Masons are admitted. The appeal of the entire sequence is one and the same throughout, an allegory of human life considered as pilgrimage and warfare, with a reward at the end in Christ for those who have walked after His commandments under the standard of Christian Chivalry.

We have very little need to make a choice between them, either on the score of antiquity or that of Ritual appeal. A descent from the Knights Templar is of course implied throughout, but it is possible to accept this, not indeed according to the literal and historical sense, but in that of the relation of symbols. The old Chivalry was founded and existed to defend the Church and its Hallows, and Masonic Knights Templar are dedicated to the same ends though official obedience's alter and Hallows transform. The Holy Sepulchre for them is the Church of Christ, however understood, and if there is anything in the old notion that the Christian Chivalry in the past had sounded strange wells of doctrine, far in the holy East, there are such wells awaiting our own exploration, to the extent that we can enter into the life behind doctrine, and this is the life which is in Christ. Finally, the modern chivalry is of Masons as well as Templars, because in both Orders there is a quest to follow and attain. But this Quest is one, a Quest for the Word, which is Christ, and a Quest for the Abodes of the Blessed, where the Word and the Soul are one.

The Morality of the Lost Word

With a measure of light and a measure of shade,
The world of old by the Word was made;
By the shade and light was the Word conceal'd,
And the Word in flesh to the world reveal'd
Is by outward sense and its forms obscured;
The spirit within is the long lost Word,
Besought by the world of the soul in pain
Through a world of words which are void and vain
O never while shadow and light are blended
Shall the world's Word-Quest or its woe be ended,
And never the world of its wounds made whole
Till the Word made flesh be the Word made soul!

Thank you for buying this Cornerstone book!

For over 25 years now, I've tried to provide the Masonic community with quality books on Masonic education, philosophy, and general interest. Your support means everything to us and keeps us afloat. Cornerstone is by no means a large company. We are a small family-owned operation that depends on your support.

Please visit our website and have a look at the many books we offer as well as the different categories of books.

If your lodge, Grand Lodge, research lodge, book club, or other body would like to have quality Cornerstone books to sell or distribute, write us. We can give you outstanding books, prices, and service.

Thanks again!
Michael R. Poll
Publisher

Cornerstone Book Publishers
1cornerstonebooks@gmail.com
http://cornerstonepublishers.com

www.ingramcontent.com/pod-product-compliance
Lightning Source LLC
LaVergne TN
LVHW041706060526
838201LV00043B/602